CW01654623

a little course in ...

GROWING VEG & FRUIT

a little course in ...

GROWING VEG & FRUIT

GARRICK STREET PRESS

Written by Simon Akeroyd

Jacket Designer Vanessa Hamilton
Senior Pre-production Producer Tony Phipps
DTP Delhi Sunil Sharma, Pushpak Tyagi
Special Sales Creative Project Manager Alison Donovan

First published in Great Britain in 2013 by
Dorling Kindersley Limited, 80 Strand, London WC2R 0RL

This 2019 edition is published by Garrick Street Press, an imprint of Dorling Kindersley Limited

001–1882150–Jan/2019

A CIP catalogue record for this book is available from the British Library.

ISBN 978-0-2413-9146-4

Contents

1 Start Simple

2 Build On It

3 Take It Further

Build Your Course

This book is divided into three sections: Start Simple, Build On It, and Take It Further. These chapters are carefully structured to help you learn new skills and techniques and then cement your increasing knowledge by completing the 22 projects.

Getting Started

You can grow crops whether you have a large allotment or just a windowbox, but the key to success is understanding your site before you start. The introduction to this book guides you through different soils and composts, shows you where you can sow and plant, and tells you how to prepare your soil. It also shows you the equipment you'll need to keep your plants healthy.

Planting Symbols

These symbols indicate what growing conditions your plant needs: sunshine or shade, or moist or light soil.

These are given at the start of each project

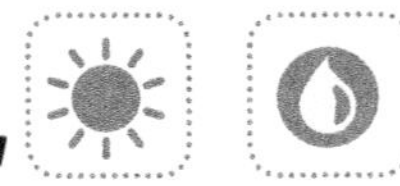

full sun **moist soil**

Key Techniques

At the beginning and end of each section are the techniques you'll need to know so that you can complete your projects successfully. They range from learning how to sow seeds and pot on seedlings to planning your own kitchen garden and making compost.

1 In every project, illustrated step-by-step text guides you carefully through the process of sowing, planting, nurturing, and harvesting your crops. The text explains in detail exactly how you need to care for your plants.

Careful! To guide you and give further useful advice, key information about each step is flagged up, preventing you making common mistakes.

Details about each task are pointed out

Caring for your **Plants**

These handy boxes are filled with troubleshooting tips and ongoing care advice so that you can keep your crops healthy and productive as they grow.

The needs of each plant are flagged up

Annotation tells you when your crop will be ready to harvest

Things to watch out for...

The "Care" boxes appear at the end of each project and list the key problems that the crop might face, whether that be a tendency to attract slugs and snails or a need for constantly moist soil. Practical advice is given to help you prevent or resolve these problems. This box also contains any other relevant information relating to the care of your plant, such as harvesting or pruning.

Now turn over to find out more ▸▸▸

Essential **Equipment**

MUST-HAVE TOOLS

Although growing your own crops isn't difficult there are a few bits of equipment that every gardener needs, such as a watering can and trowel. Invest in the best-quality tools you can afford – not only will they last well over time, but they will be a pleasure to use every time you step into your garden.

Watering can
The fine rose nozzle distributes the flow of water so that it doesn't damage young, delicate seedlings

Dibber
Used to create planting holes, a dibber is pushed into the soil to the appropriate depth

Hand fork
This tool allows you to be more precise when digging weeds and lifting plants than if using a large fork

Trowel
Create neat planting holes in the soil with this tool and use to harvest crops such as garlic

Hoe
Use to weed around your crops by lifting the soil and chopping through weeds. Long-handled types are also available

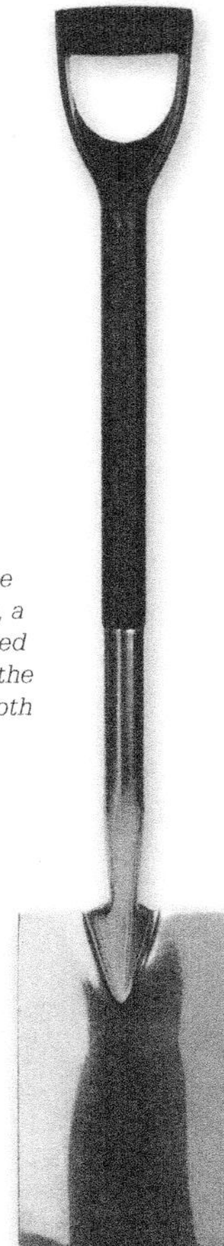

Spade
Essential for lifting and moving soil or mulches and digging grit or compost in

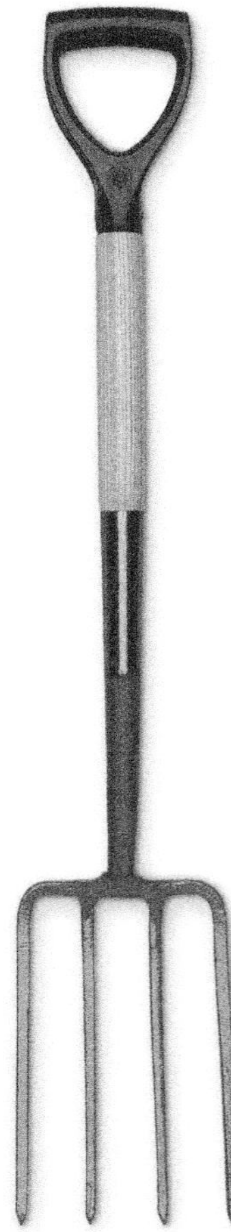

Fork
Lift weeds, turn the soil over, and harvest root crops using a long-handled fork

Rake
Use this tool to level the soil and break it down to a fine texture before sowing and planting

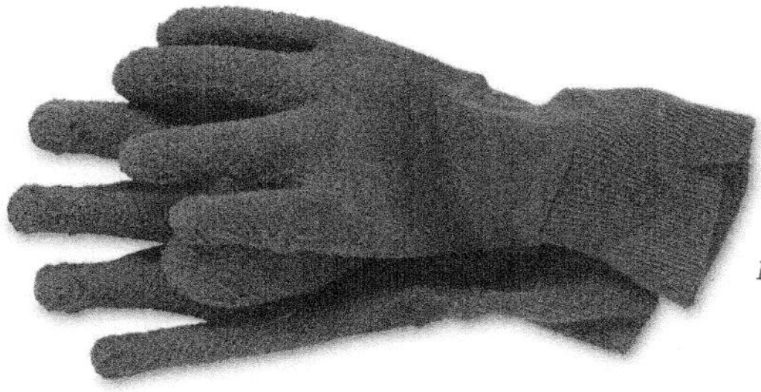

Gloves
Protect your hands when using fertilizers or insecticides and when pruning thorny plants

Scissors
Use to harvest cut-and-come-again salad crops and snip garden string to size

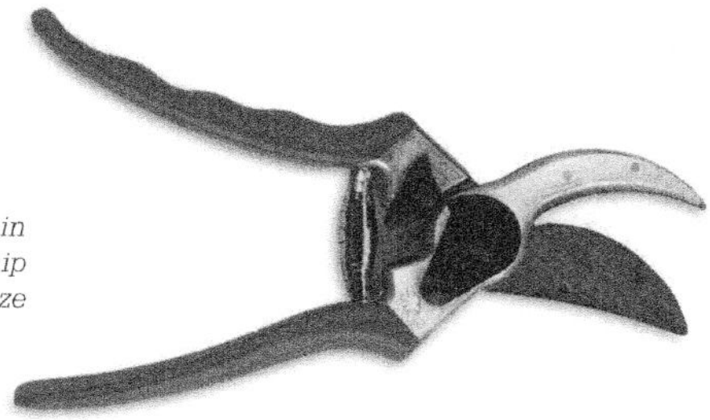

Drill
Use to create drainage holes in pots and attach sturdy brackets for hanging baskets

Secateurs
The sturdy blades are essential for pruning fruiting shrubs and trees and harvesting crops with woody stems

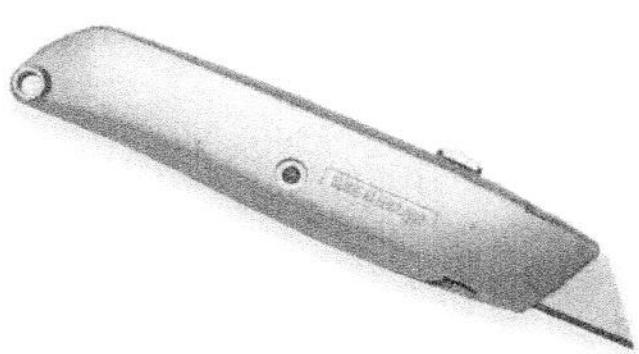

Seed Markers
Mark your pots and drills with these so that you don't get your seedlings mixed up

Stanley knife
Use this sharp blade to create clean-cut planting holes when laying weed-suppressing fabrics

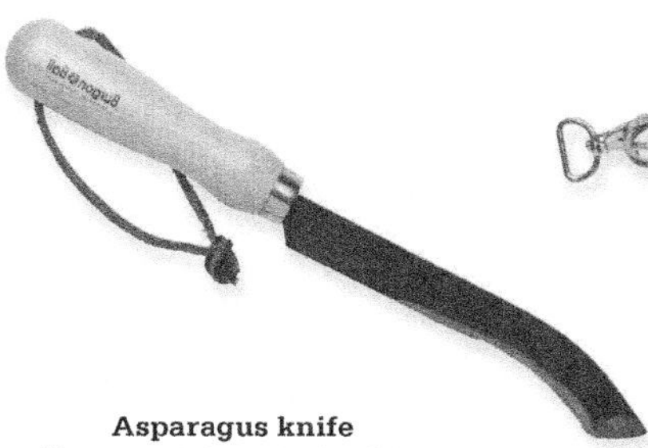

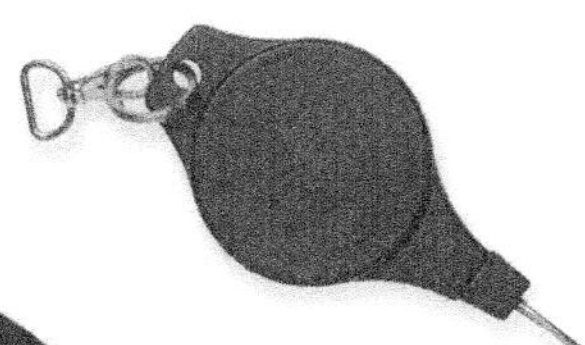

Asparagus knife
The curved sharp blade of this tool makes it useful for harvesting the spears of asparagus close to ground level

Tape measure
Essential for ensuring that your seedlings have enough space between them

ESSENTIAL EXTRAS

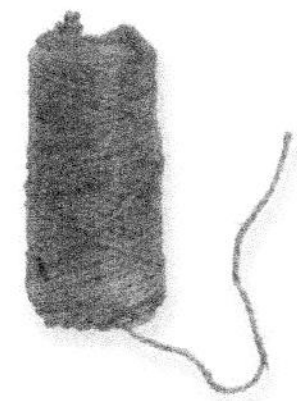

Canes and string
Support tall or top-heavy plants by tying them to sturdy stakes or canes

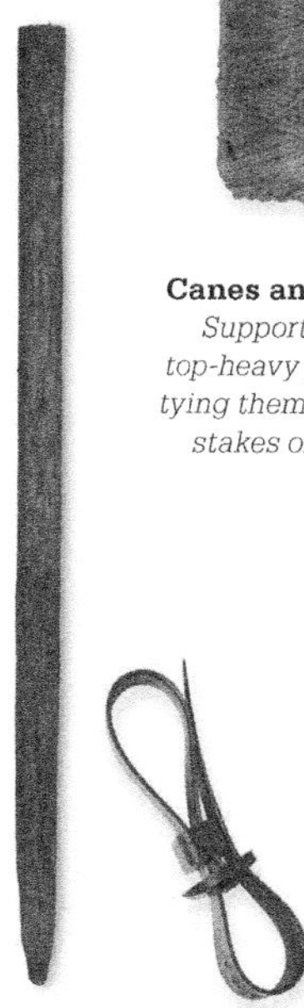

Tree stake and tie
Use a stake and tie to keep fruit trees upright – the extendable ties give the trunks room to swell

Essential **Equipment** *continued*

CONTAINERS

From small plastic pots that can be kept warm on a window ledge while seeds germinate to large, frost-proof tubs for fruit trees, there are containers to suit your crops at all stages of growth. Just make sure they have holes in the bottom and place crocks in the base to help with drainage.

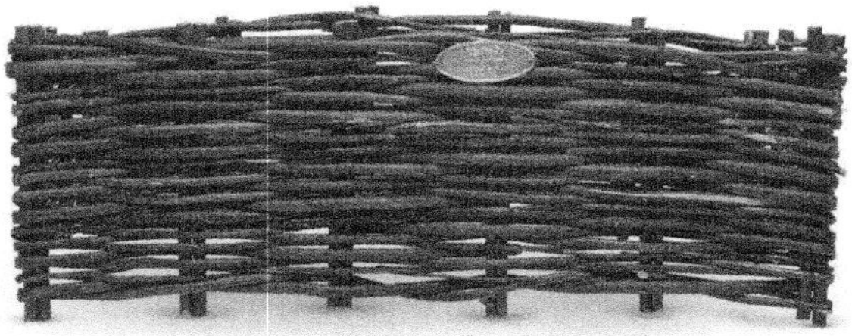

Windowbox
These enable you to grow crops on a windowsill so that they are easy to harvest. A range of styles is available

Terracotta pots
These attractive pots make a lovely garden feature, but are porous and drain fairly quickly

Plastic pots
Cheap and cheerful, these pots are ideal for seed sowing and are available in a range of sizes

Module trays
Sow seeds in the compartments or "modules" of these trays so that the seedlings are easy to move once they develop

Biodegradable pots and modules
Sow seeds in these and once the plants begin to grow, plant the pots into the ground – this removes the need to lift plants and risk disturbing their roots

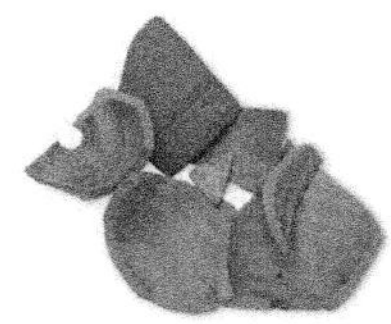

Crocks
Place pieces of terracotta in the bottom of containers to help the soil to drain

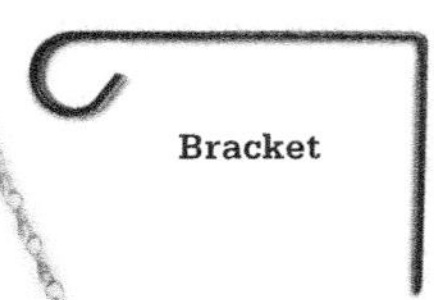

Bracket

Trug
Use a deep container for root crops or large plants – trugs, bins, or planting bags make great growing locations

Hanging basket
Create a hanging display of crops in a basket that is attached to a sturdy surface, such as a wall or fence

EXTRA HELP

Sometimes your crops may need a bit of extra help and protection if temperatures drop or weeds and pests threaten, while some tender crops such as peppers won't even consider germinating unless you give them a warm environment after sowing. These essential items will make it easy for you to keep crops healthy and happy as they grow.

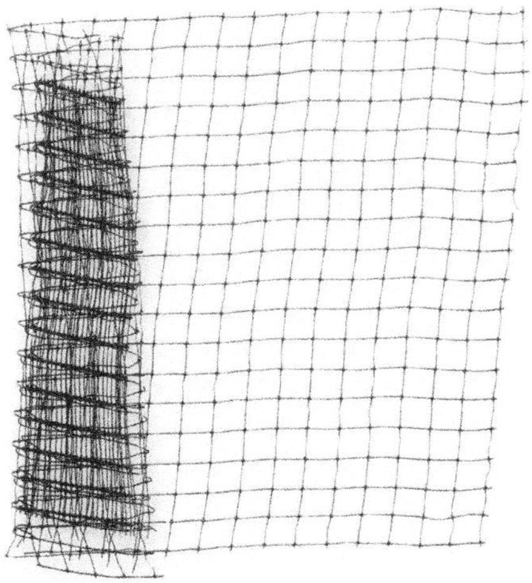

Netting
Use netting anchored at the base of plants to keep out large pests such as birds. Finer, insect-proof mesh will protect plants from pests such as cabbage white butterflies

Fleece
If frosts are threatened, use horticultural fleece to protect tender plants or the blossom of plum and cherry trees from damage – simply lay it over your crops

Black landscape fabric
This fabric can be laid on the ground before planting as it helps to warm the soil, control weed growth, and retain soil moisture. Cut holes and plant your crops through it

Propagator
A propagator provides a warm environment for seeds that need higher temperatures to germinate, and young seedlings. Choose heated models or simple plastic structures

Compost and soil types

To be successful in the vegetable garden you need to provide suitable growing conditions for your crops: the soil must contain enough nutrients and drain well. Ideal conditions vary from crop to crop, but there is a wide range of composts that can be used if you are growing plants in pots, and if your soil is heavy or very sandy you can improve it by digging in compost or well-rotted manure.

General-purpose compost

General-purpose compost is a useful soil improver and can be dug into your soil to improve its bulk and ability to retain moisture. It can also be used in containers, hanging baskets, or even for seed sowing, but is prone to drying out quickly. There are a number of different types, containing varying ratios of peat, loam, sand, and fertilizers, so read the instructions and choose the one that will best support the crops you want to grow.

Seed compost

Seed compost is often soil-based, making it heavier than general-purpose compost and much better at retaining moisture. Its fine texture makes it ideal for seed sowing, either in individual pots or in module trays. Seed compost does contain some nutrients, but in fairly low quantities, which suits emerging seedlings in the early stages of development. Some companies also produce composts for "potting on" and "pricking out".

Ericaceous compost

This compost has a low pH making it suitable for crops that thrive in acidic conditions, such as blueberries and cranberries. It can either be added to raised or sunken beds to increase the acidity of the existing soil or used to fill containers. Like general-purpose compost, it can quickly dry out and will need watering regularly if in containers. Take care to water this compost using rainwater, as regular tap water will alter its pH.

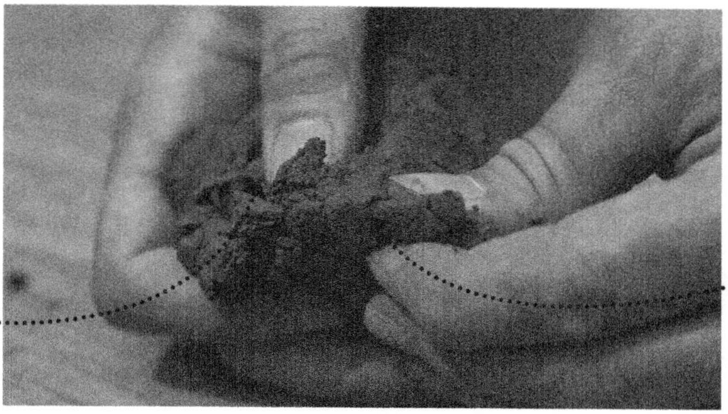

Testing a clay soil

Clay Soil

To test if your soil is clay-based, roll it into a ball. If the ball stays intact without crumbling it is clay. Digging clay soils can be back-breaking work: in dry periods clay can bake as hard as a brick while in wet weather it may be too sticky and heavy to work with. However, clay is also very fertile and easily gives up its nutrients. The dense structure of clay means that it doesn't drain very well, so dig in grit, sand, and organic matter to improve its drainage. Plants that prefer heavy soils include cabbages, Brussels sprouts, and broccoli.

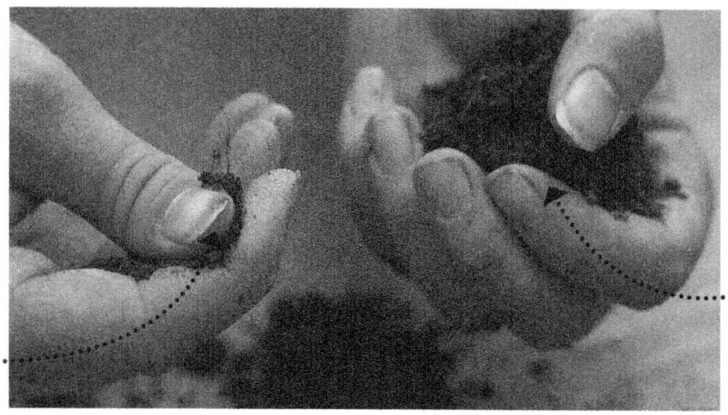

Testing a sandy soil

Sandy Soil

If the soil crumbles easily between your fingers it contains a high quantity of sand. Digging sandy soil is easy. It is light and free-draining, which means that plants are less likely to rot or pick up fungal diseases in wet weather. However, sand is low in nutrients and doesn't retain much moisture, making watering a full time job in summer. To improve the soil, dig in well-rotted manure or compost and apply fertilizers regularly to supply plants with nutrients. Vegetables that prefer lighter, sandy soils include carrots and parsnips.

pH testing

Testing to see if your soil is acidic or alkaline is important, as a few crops need specific pH levels. Growing a crop in the wrong pH leads to nutrient deficiencies, as it can't extract what it needs from the soil. Blueberries, for example, will only thrive in acid soil so it would be a waste of money to plant them up in an alkaline soil that will eventually kill them. If you're unsure of your soil's pH, a simple testing kit can be purchased from garden centres. Soil conditions will only change very gradually, so it is only necessary to test every few years.

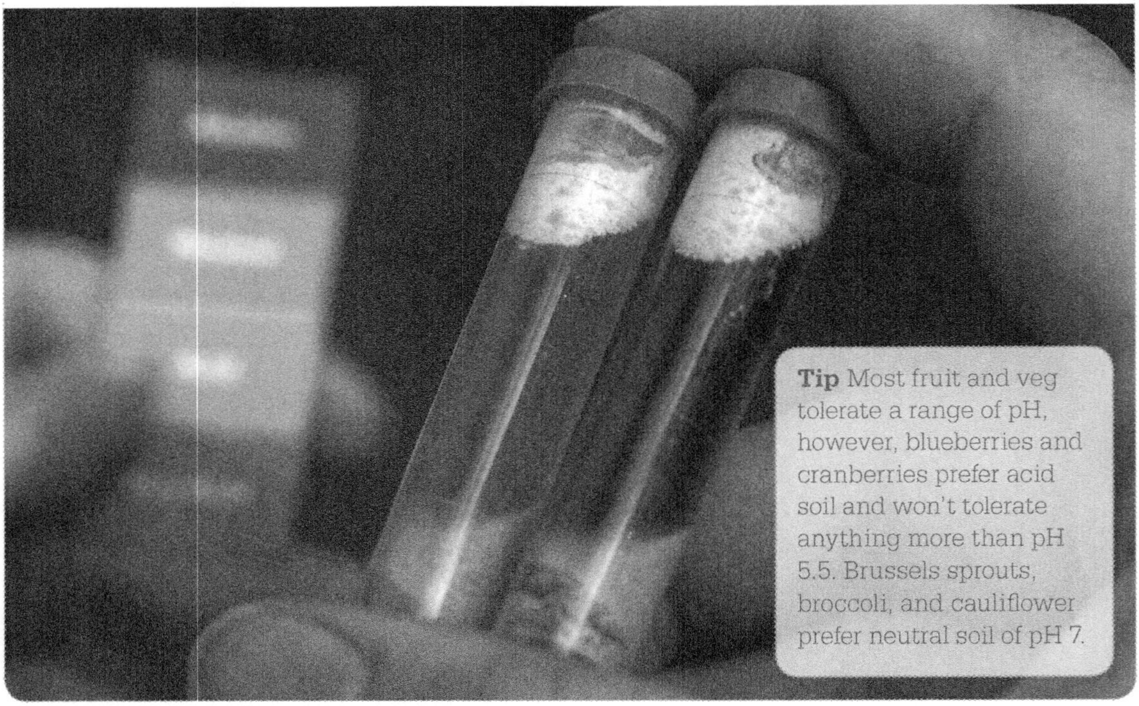

Tip Most fruit and veg tolerate a range of pH, however, blueberries and cranberries prefer acid soil and won't tolerate anything more than pH 5.5. Brussels sprouts, broccoli, and cauliflower prefer neutral soil of pH 7.

Controlling conditions

If your soil doesn't suit the crops you want to grow it is possible to alter the pH. Lime can be added to make conditions more alkaline, and ericaceous compost, sulphur chips, or rotted pine needles can be dug in to make it more acidic. However, this will only have a temporary effect on the soil and these products will eventually wash away. The simplest solution to soils with extreme pH is to grow crops in containers and raised beds. This way you can use an appropriate compost and control the conditions more easily.

Preparing your soil

Before planting, you will need to thoroughly prepare your soil. Put the effort in at this stage, because later it will become difficult to rid the beds of deep-rooted weeds or compacted soil. All your hard work will be well rewarded, as your plants should thrive in these conditions.

1 If you are taking on a new allotment or have recently moved house, there may be rubbish such as bricks and rubble littering the ground. Clear the ground of all debris, and if you need to, use a strimmer to cut back large swathes of weeds. Dig out any weeds using a fork, as a spade will slice through the roots and encourage them to multiply.

Try to remove weeds in one piece to avoid leaving bits behind that could regrow

Lever deep roots out using your fork

2 Once you have cleared all rubble and weeds, the next stage is to thoroughly dig over the soil. Using a spade will help you to dig deeply, breaking up any compaction or large clods of soil below the surface that could impede the roots. Use a fork to lift the soil and sift it. Ideally try to dig down to twice the depth of the spade or fork.

3 Once the soil has been dug over, dig in some organic matter. The best material to use is home-made garden compost, but you can also buy it from the garden centre. Contact your local stables as they may deliver well-rotted manure. After adding the organic matter, the soil should be raked level and left to settle for a few weeks before you plant any crops.

Make sure that compost is well-rotted as otherwise it can scorch crops

Use a fork to lightly dig the organic material into the soil

Growing locations

Growing your own crops is simple. You don't need an orchard, an allotment, or even a huge garden. Most crops can be grown in pots, windowboxes, and raised beds, allowing you to grow tasty produce in spaces as small as patios, balconies, and roof gardens. You could even get creative and grow crops in old welly boots, tupperware, or even an old kitchen sink.

Tip You can use almost anything you like as a container, but you must make sure that there are holes in the bottom for excess water to drain out through.

Containers

Containers are a great choice for growing crops: they can be moved during the season to ensure sunlight reaches all sides, and weeding is simple as there is hardly any bare soil to cultivate. Choose frost-resistant outdoor pots and consider the size carefully before sowing – some crops such as carrots will need a deeper pot than shallow rooted plants such as lettuce. As pots drain faster than the open ground you will need to remember to water the plants regularly and give them a weekly liquid feed.

Windowboxes

If you want to make the most of your outdoor space and you have a window ledge to spare, consider growing crops in a windowbox. They are ideal placed outside the kitchen so that you can easily harvest a handful of fresh herbs or salad leaves while you are cooking. Make regular sowings all year round to ensure that there is always something tasty to harvest within reach.

Raised beds

Raised beds

A raised bed is the perfect solution if you have poor-quality soil as you can simply start afresh and fill it with rich new compost. The extra height means that the soil will drain well and warm up quickly in spring, while crops will be at a more convenient height to harvest. Raised beds can be made from recycled timber such as sleepers or gravel boards but if you're not sure your DIY skills are up to the challenge there are lots of raised-bed kits available.

Srawberry boots

Unusual locations

Be imaginative with where you grow your next meal. Recycle materials such as old kettles, juice cartons, and colanders to use as containers. Even old gardening boots can be filled with soil and planted with trailing crops such as strawberries. Larger items such as old wheelbarrows or an old kitchen sink could also make an excellent growing environment – just make sure that whatever you use has drainage holes in the base.

Choosing a site

Before you get started with sowing or planting it's worth taking the time to get to know your plot. Figure out which areas are bathed in sunlight and which parts are often in shade. Check this at different times of the day as the sun moves across the sky. Also check to see where the prevailing wind is and identify whether there are any areas of ground that are prone to frost.

Sun-loving squashes

Shade-loving Swiss chard

Sunshine and shade

While crops that are grown in pots can be moved between sunshine and shade to suit, those that are grown in the ground do not have this luxury and must be planted in a suitable location. Most plants prefer full sun – for example, Mediterranean-type plants such as tomatoes, aubergines, peppers, and squashes should be planted where they won't be shaded by other plants. However, don't despair if you have a shady site as some plants will tolerate light or even full shade. Leafy crops like Swiss chard and spinach, along with members of the cabbage family, such as Brussels sprouts, broccoli, and cauliflower, will generally tolerate moderate shade. Cooking apples, gooseberries, and redcurrants will grow on cool, north-facing walls, while rhubarb is ideal for smothering weeds in shady corners of the garden.

Sheltered sites

Strong winds can knock over tall plants such as sweetcorn and shred the leaves of leafy crops. Particularly fierce gusts can also damage fruit trees by causing them to rock in the soil, which damages their roots. If your site is particularly exposed you may want to create windbreaks to prevent this happening. The most useful type of protection is a hedge as it slows the wind but doesn't block it completely. Air movement is important as it prevents the build-up of pests and diseases. Consider using bulky plants such as rows of runner beans or blackberry bushes to protect your more tender crops. Alternatively, plant a mixed hedge from hawthorn, elder, wild roses, and blackthorn, as this is great for wildlife.

Frost protection

Frosts do most of their damage in spring, when young tender crops are planted out and buds and blossom start to emerge on fruit trees and bushes. There are various methods of protection but the most common is to cover plants with a cloche – a cloche is polythene covering that is placed over crops to keep them warm. Fleeces can also be draped over fruit trees or laid over recently sown vegetables. Always listen to the weather forecast and be patient, waiting until the risk of frosts are over before planting out.

The science of The Life Cycle of Plants

Understanding the key stages in a plant's growth cycle is essential to becoming a good gardener. A plant's main concern is to produce seed so that it can reproduce. Seed is dispersed by various methods including wind, animals, water, or of course, by gardeners.

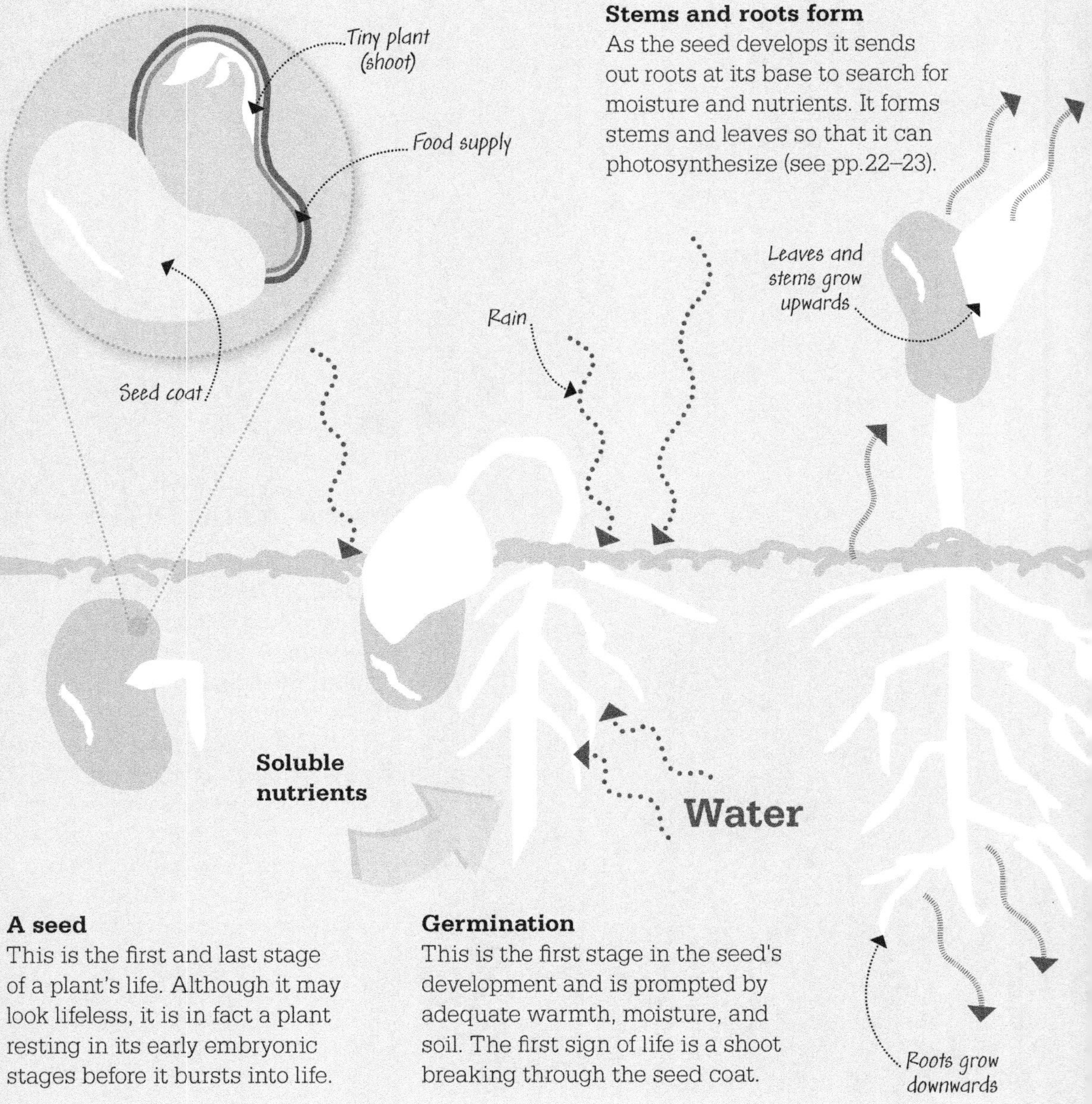

Stems and roots form
As the seed develops it sends out roots at its base to search for moisture and nutrients. It forms stems and leaves so that it can photosynthesize (see pp.22–23).

A seed
This is the first and last stage of a plant's life. Although it may look lifeless, it is in fact a plant resting in its early embryonic stages before it bursts into life.

Germination
This is the first stage in the seed's development and is prompted by adequate warmth, moisture, and soil. The first sign of life is a shoot breaking through the seed coat.

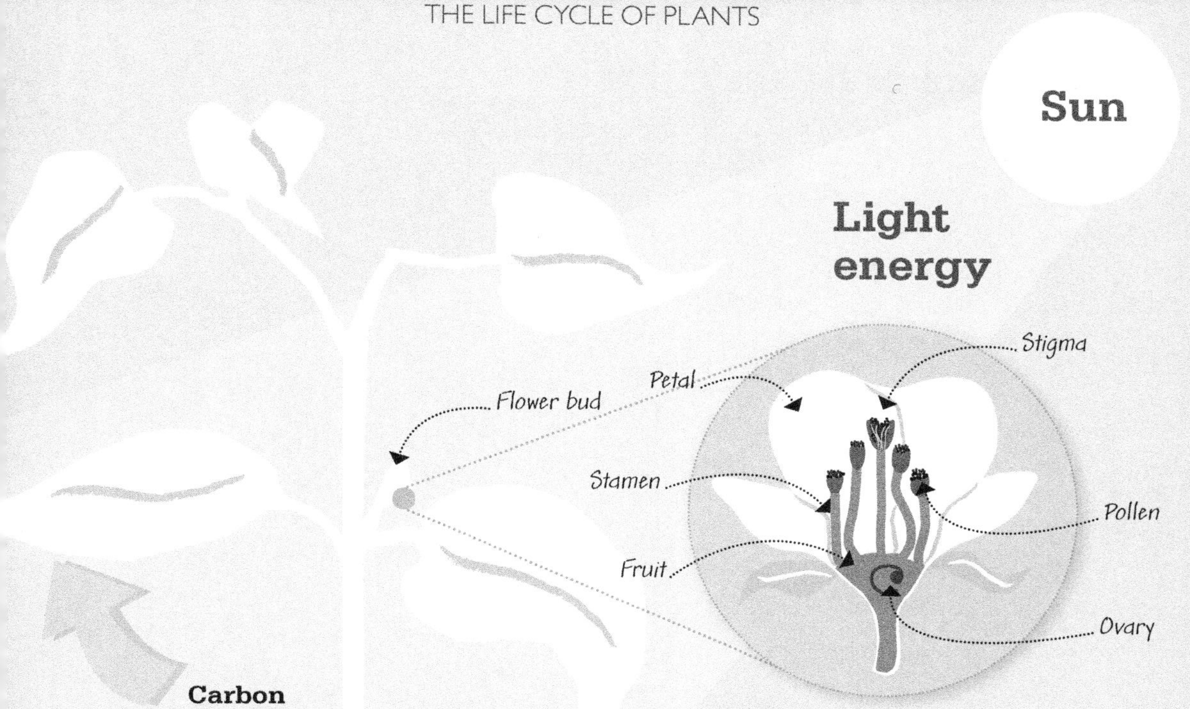

Flowers form
To produce fruits and seeds, flowers must be fertilized by pollinating insects. The more colourful and scented the flower the more insects it will attract.

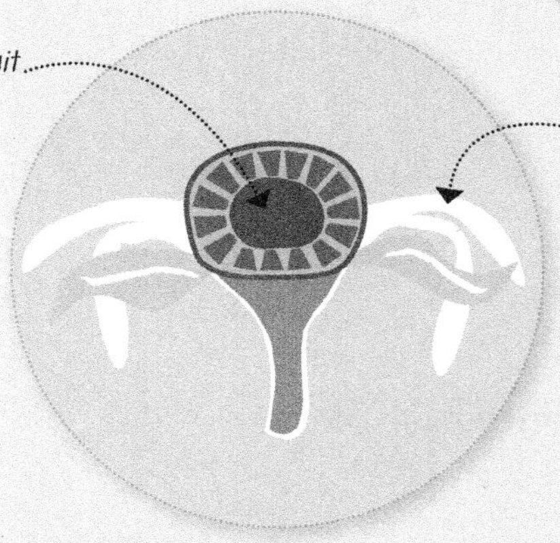

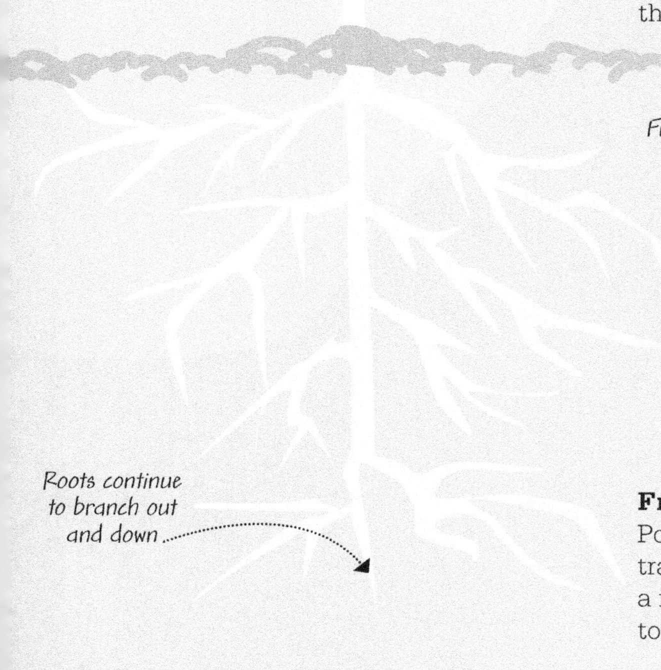

Fruits develop
Pollination occurs when pollen is transferred from a male stamen onto a female stigma. The ovary swells to become the seed-filled fruit.

The science of Photosynthesis

This is the essential process by which plants create their food and energy. Without this they wouldn't be able to grow. The key raw ingredients are light, water, and carbon dioxide, which are converted into sugar and oxygen. Carbon dioxide is received from the air through their leaves, light is received via the sun, while water is obtained through their roots.

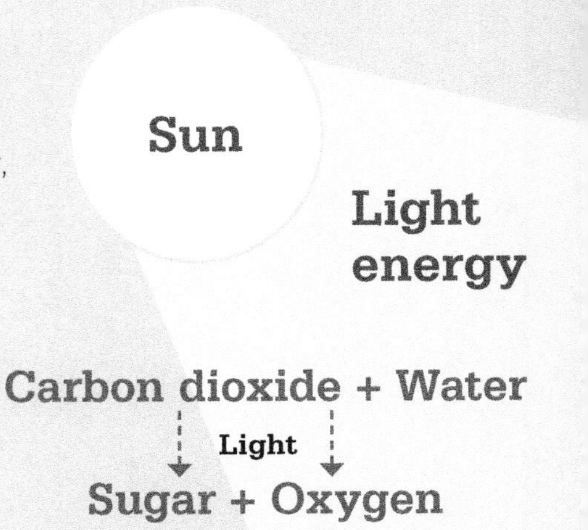

The movement of carbon dioxide
Plants take in carbon dioxide from the air. The carbon dioxide diffuses into the leaves through tiny holes in the underside of the leaf called stomata (see below, right).

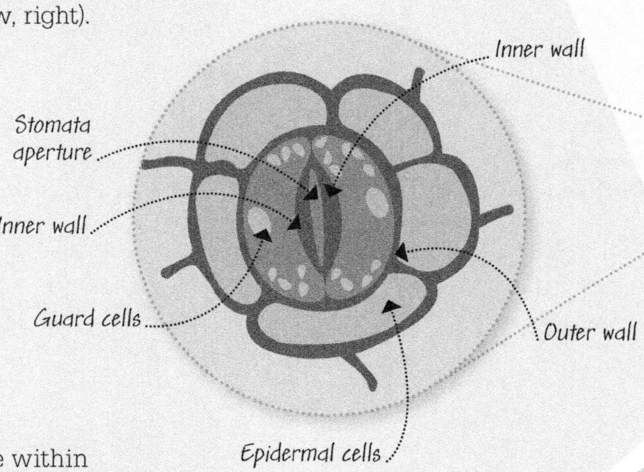

Cell structure
Photosynthesis takes place within the plant's cells in structures called chloroplasts. These contain chlorophyll, the green pigment that gives the leaves and stems their colour.

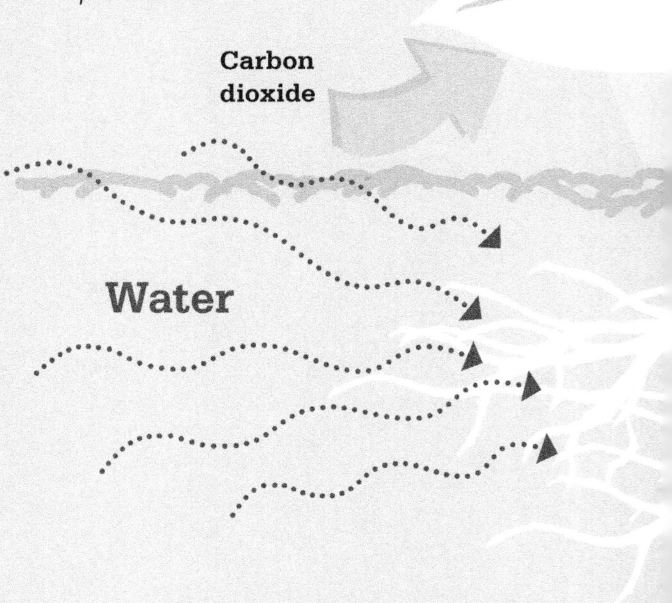

The movement of water
Plants get the water they need for photosynthesis by absorbing it through their roots. It is drawn up the plant and into the leaves through tubes in the stem known as xylems.

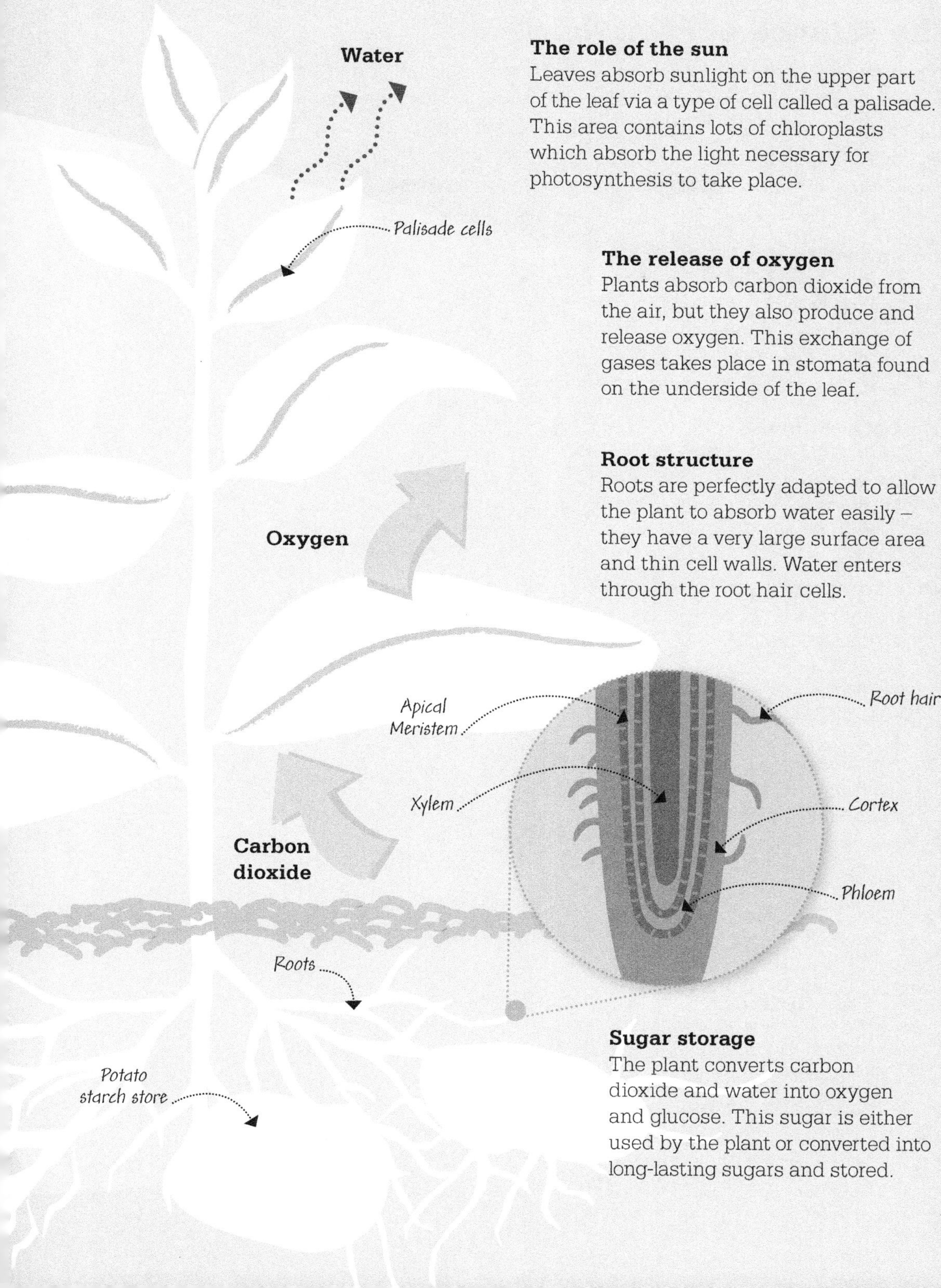

The role of the sun
Leaves absorb sunlight on the upper part of the leaf via a type of cell called a palisade. This area contains lots of chloroplasts which absorb the light necessary for photosynthesis to take place.

The release of oxygen
Plants absorb carbon dioxide from the air, but they also produce and release oxygen. This exchange of gases takes place in stomata found on the underside of the leaf.

Root structure
Roots are perfectly adapted to allow the plant to absorb water easily – they have a very large surface area and thin cell walls. Water enters through the root hair cells.

Sugar storage
The plant converts carbon dioxide and water into oxygen and glucose. This sugar is either used by the plant or converted into long-lasting sugars and stored.

The science of Plant Needs

Plants won't grow properly if they don't get the right nutrients. Most nutrients are taken up from the soil, so you can give your plant a boost by adding fertilizers and soil improvers to your garden. Others reach the plant via the air and water, which is why it's so important to keep plants well watered.

Structural nutrients
Carbon, hydrogen, and oxygen are found in the air and water. They are known as structural nutrients as they help to build cellulose, which keeps plants strong and upright. They also contribute to the photosynthesis process.

Primary macro-nutrients
The three essential nutrients a plant needs are nitrogen, phosphorus, and potassium. They are found in the soil and are abbreviated to NPK when referred to in fertilizer.

Secondary macro-nutrients
Sulphur, calcium, and magnesium are the next most important elements. Soils are not often lacking in these nutrients and levels of calcium and magnesium are increased when lime has been added.

Micro-nutrients
These nutrients are only needed in tiny amounts. They include elements such as boron, copper, manganese, iron, and zinc.

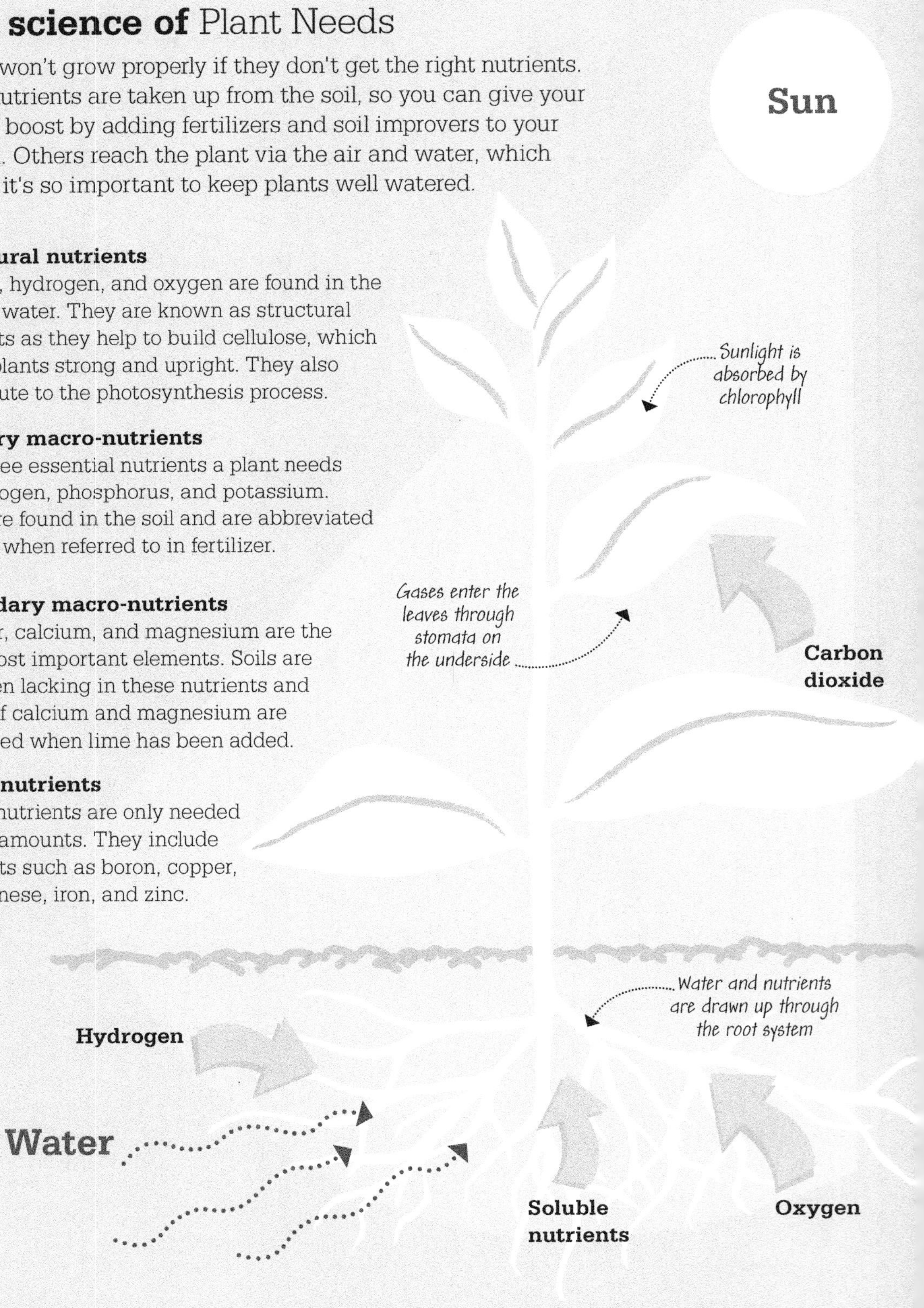

Nutrient	*What it does*	*What happens if the plant doesn't have enough*	*Where it comes from*
Carbon	In photosynthesis it becomes converted to sugar in the plant	The plant won't be able to produce energy for itself and dies	It is taken from carbon dioxide from the surrounding air
Hydrogen	Needed for building up sugars during photosynthesis	The lack of hydrogen results in lack of sugar and the plant dies	It is obtained from the air or from water
Oxygen	Is needed for the plant to convert the sugar it has made into energy	It would be unlikely for a plant to be depleted of oxygen	It comes from the surrounding air and from water
Nitrogen	Helps the plant to produce green, lush growth and foliage	Plant growth stops and the leaves turn yellow, starting at the bottom	The soil and fertilizers; legumes fix it from the atmosphere
Phosphorus	It stimulates healthy root growth and rapid growth in plants	Roots don't develop and foliage turns purplish, starting at the bottom	The soil, but also found in fertilizers, such as blood, fish, and bone
Potassium	Promotes colour, flavour, and resistance to disease	Yellowing and sometimes spotting on the lower leaves	It is found in the soil and often added to fertilizers
Sulphur	Promotes chlorophyll formation, root growth, vigour, and hardiness	The plant develops yellow leaves and spindly growth,	In the soil, usually from rainwater, also in many fertilizers
Calcium	Forms part of the plant cell wall structure and strengthens the plant	Yellowing at the most active sections of plant, such as the leaf tips	In the soil, but also from lime, gypsum, and super-sulphate
Magnesium	Forms chlorophyll and is needed for photosynthesis	The leaves start to turn yellow between the veins	In the soil and from organic material, fertilizers, and lime
Iron	Key in the development of chlorophyll and the photosynthesis process	Deficiency causes a yellowing around the edge of the foliage	Found in the soil but also common in fertilizers
Zinc	Helps to control and regulate the consumption of sugars	A deficiency causes malformed leaves or fruit	Found in the soil but is also common in fertilizers
Manganese	It assists in the breakdown of sugars for the plant	The leaves start to turn yellow between the veins	It is commonly found in the soil
Copper	Aids growth and helps with the metabolism of sugars	The plant develops yellowing in the upper leaves	Found in the soil and in fertilizers

1

Start Simple

Growing your own fruit and vegetables is an incredibly rewarding experience. Once you've mastered the basics and learned how to give plants the care they need, there's a large number of crops to choose from, even if you only have a small garden. This chapter starts you off with some of the easiest and most reliable crops, from fresh leafy salads, to sweet and juicy strawberries.

In this section learn to grow:

Salad leaves
see pp.36–39

Tomatoes
see pp.42–45

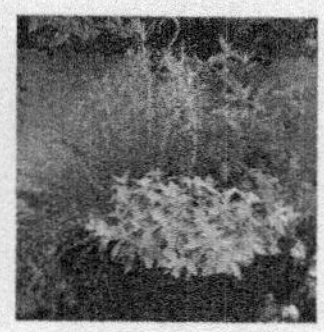

Herbs
see pp.48–51

Onions
see pp.52–55

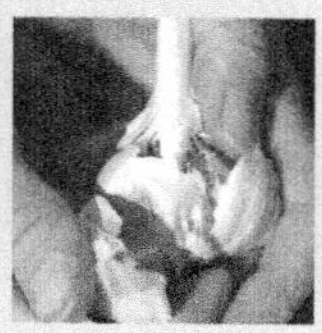

Garlic
see pp.56–59

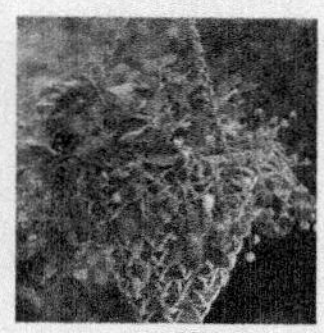

Strawberries
see pp.60–64

How to **Sow Seeds**

Seeing the young shoots of crops you've sown is always exciting. Seeds can be bought from your local garden centre or online, or simply collected from plants grown the previous year. Some crops can be sown directly outdoors, others will need to be started off indoors.

Tip Some crops simply won't survive if they are sown straight into the ground outdoors, as they need protection from cold temperatures while they are young. Following the instructions on the seed packet, start them off inside in trays or pots.

Sowing in trays

For tiny seeds, such as lettuces, fill a seed tray with compost and lightly firm down. Scatter the seeds over the surface, then lightly cover them with more compost. Water and cover the tray with glass or a clear plastic lid and keep in a warm, light place, such as on a windowsill, to allow the seeds to germinate. Remove the cover as soon as shoots appear.

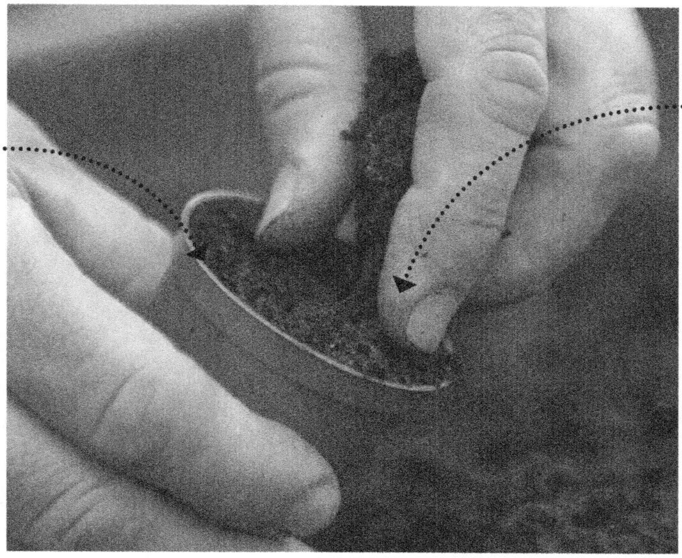

Fill the pot with compost

Cover the seed with compost

Sowing in pots

Larger seeds, such as runner beans, can be sown into individual pots. Fill the pots with general-purpose compost and make a planting hole using a dibber or your finger. Drop one seed into each hole and cover with compost. Always water the seeds after sowing. Cover each pot with a plastic bag, tied on with a rubber band, until the first shoots appear.

How to **Plant Out**

Whether you have grown your own plants from seeds or bought them from the garden centre, timing is everything when it comes to planting them outdoors. Plant them out too early and they may get frost-damaged; too late and they could become pot bound and unhealthy.

Tip If you have limited space and lots of seedlings, discard the unhealthy, smaller plants and just focus on planting out the strongest ones.

Taking a plant out of its pot

Gently remove the plant from its pot by lightly squeezing the base with one hand, taking care not to damage the roots. Use your other hand to hold the plant carefully by the base of the stem, making sure that it doesn't bend or break. For tray-grown seeds, hold the seedling gently by its leaves and tease out its fragile roots with a dibber or blunt pencil.

Planting in the ground

Dig a hole the same depth as the pot and line the base with compost. Be careful not to plant too deeply, or the stem will start to rot. However, if not planted deep enough, the root ball will quickly dry out and start to wilt. Firm the plant into the soil with your fingertips after planting.

Watering in

Use a rose fitting on your watering can to sprinkle water gently around your new plant – this way you can give it a thorough soaking without risking damage to its leaves or stem. Watering the plant in well will help the roots settle into the new soil.

How to **Water Your Plants**

Water is vital to keep your plants alive and healthy, so it is essential that you do not let them dry out. However, it is also important to try to conserve water in the garden. Use water butts to collect rainwater and water the plants in the morning or evening when the temperature is coolest so that the plants can absorb the water before it evaporates.

Watering cans

There are many methods for watering plants. A watering can is ideal if you have a small plot or a collection of pots close to your house. It is a little harder work if your vegetable garden is a long way from the tap or water butt, but may be the only way if a hosepipe ban is in place.

Aim the hose towards the base of the plants, to avoid damaging them

This attachment has a long handle, making it easy to reach far away plants

Hosepipes

Using a hosepipe is an easy and efficient way to water your crops. Many hosepipes have attachment heads with a range of different settings, which allow you to accurately control the placement and amount of water you are giving to your plants.

Water seeps directly into the soil through holes in a hosepipe

Regular watering will keep your plants green and healthy

Drip hoses

Drip or seep hoses have tiny perforations in the piping through which a regular or controlled supply of water goes directly to your plants' roots, where it is most needed. Laid on the ground, these hoses keep the soil moist, encouraging your vegetables to grow.

How to **Tie In and Pinch Out**

Some crops have a natural tendency to use their energy to grow large and leafy rather than produce plump fruit and vegetables, but there are ways to control this. Rampant growth can be kept under control by tying in the plants, keeping them neat and easy to manage. At other times, plants may need their shoots pinched out to redirect their growth.

Tip When tying in plants, use a soft twine and tie them to a sturdy stake with a figure-of-eight knot. This technique creates space for the stem to swell as it grows. It also stops the stem from rubbing against the cane.

Tying in

Plants such as tomatoes, aubergines, and peppers need to be regularly tied in, as they grow quickly through the summer months. Use a sturdy stake to keep them upright and in place. Remember, too, that as their fruits grow heavier they will need a lot of support.

Pinching out sideshoots

Pinching out the growing tips

Pinching out

There are two reasons for pinching out a plant. First, pinching out sideshoots on plants such as tomatoes ensures that their energy goes into producing fruit rather than leaves. Second, pinching out the growing tips of leaf crops, such as basil, encourages bushier growth.

Grow Salad in a Windowbox

Growing salad in a windowbox is easy and gives quick, delicious results – it will also be much cheaper than buying bags of supermarket salad. Because the leaves are close at hand it is easy to keep an eye on them to make sure they don't dry out, and they are ideally placed for harvesting.

full sun or part shade

moist soil

Equipment

- Windowbox
- Crocks
- General-purpose compost
- Trowel
- Bamboo cane
- Packet of seeds
  such as lettuce, rocket, or lamb's lettuce
- Watering can with a fine rose
- Scissors

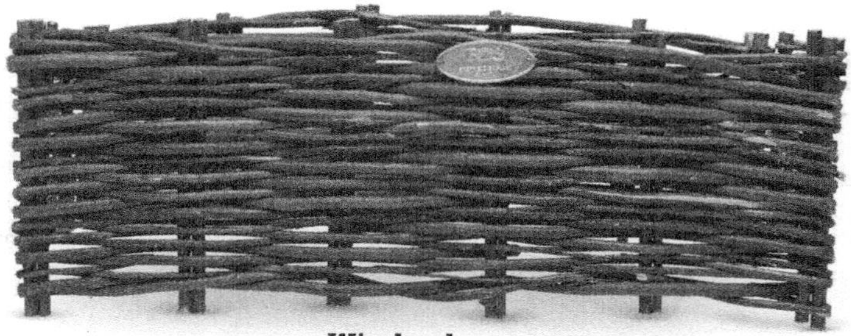
Windowbox

General-purpose compost

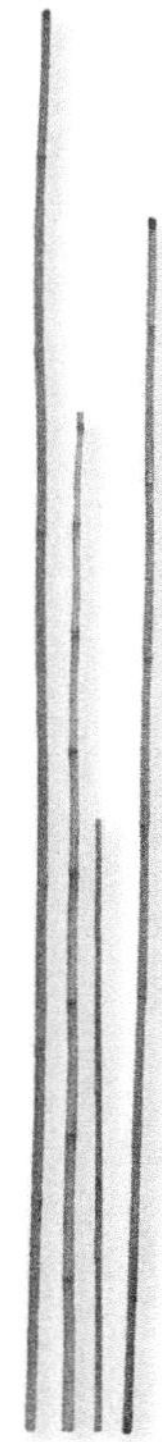
Bamboo canes

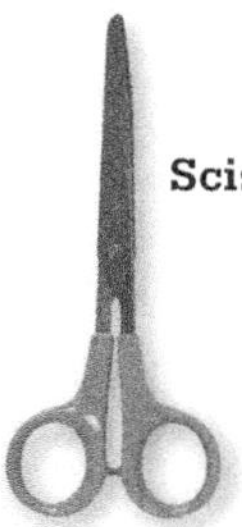
Scissors

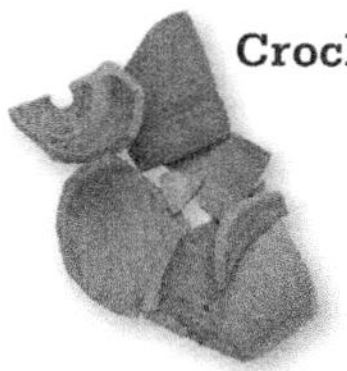
Crocks

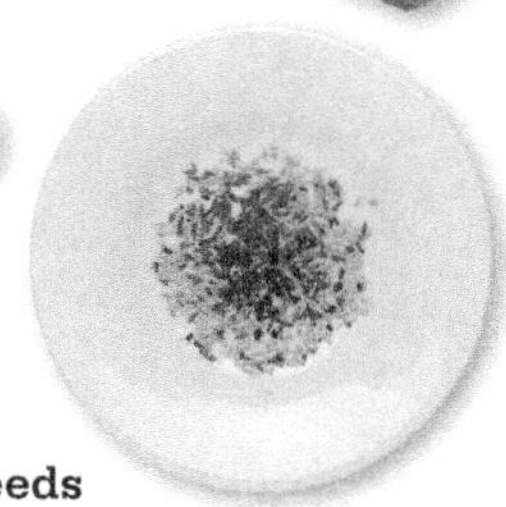
Seeds

Watering can

Trowel

Salad leaves *4–6 weeks until harvest*

Sow *all year indoors; mid-spring to early autumn outside*

Water *the seedlings well, especially in hot summer weather*

Harvest *all year indoors; mid-spring to mid-autumn outside*

1 Place crocks over the drainage holes in the bottom of the windowbox, then fill it up with good-quality general-purpose compost. Water the surface lightly using a watering can with a fine rose, then push a piece of bamboo cane lengthways into the compost to create shallow drills.

Tip Germination will be quicker if the soil is slightly damp.

2 Tip the seeds into the palm of your hand and sprinkle them into the drill at the spacing recommended on the seed packet.

Tip If the seeds are tiny, mix them with some sand – this will allow you to see where you have sown, so that you don't miss any drills or accidentally sow twice.

3 Lightly cover the seeds with compost and place on a sunny or partly shaded windowsill. Water the plants regularly to stop the soil drying out. In four to six weeks, once the leaves are ready to harvest, cut them just above the base every few days so that they can re-sprout.

Careful! The plants may need watering every day in summer, as windowboxes dry out quickly.

Caring for your **Salad Leaves**

Salad leaves are very easy to grow, but you will need to water them regularly and protect them from slugs to guarantee the very best crop.

Things to watch out for...

Wilted leaves Windowboxes drain quickly, especially when they are in a sunny position, so if your leaves are looking limp or wilted they will need a thorough soaking. Water them well and regularly check the surface of the soil to make sure it hasn't dried out. Nourish the plants with a liquid feed once a week to prevent them from running out of energy.

Slugs and snails These common garden pests can devour your salad crops, which may not be completely safe, even in a windowbox. Regularly check the plants for signs of damage and see pp.66–67 for tips on how to deal with them. Caterpillars may also attack your plants; remove them by hand as soon as you spot them.

Garden thieves If birds are a problem you may need to protect crops with a net.

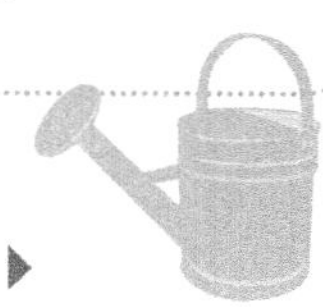

Also learn to grow ▶▶▶

How to grow **Lettuce and Edible flowers**

full sun or part shade

moist soil

Equipment

- Lettuce or edible flower seeds
- A container such as a windowbox
- General-purpose compost
- Watering can

Tender salad leaves and edible flowers, such as nasturtiums, calendula, and violas, can be grown easily in containers, and are shallow-rooted so are ideal for windowboxes. They are so quick to grow that within weeks of planting you'll be picking delicious flowerheads or succulent leaves that will add colour and flavour to your salads.

Lettuce

SOWING

Sow the seeds in spring in containers filled with general-purpose compost. Make shallow drills and sprinkle the seeds in carefully. Cover them over with compost and water in well. Once the seedlings start to show, ensure they get lots of sunlight. Water them regularly, remembering to water the compost and not the tender leaves.

Thin out the seedlings if they become crowded. If you are thinning lettuce seedlings, don't discard them; wash and add to salads as baby leaves.

HARVESTING

Lettuce should be fully grown in around 10–12 weeks, and can be harvested whole. Alternatively, harvest them as tasty cut-and-come-again crops.

Edible flowers will be ready to harvest in about 5–6 weeks. Pick the blooming flowerheads regularly and lay them out on kitchen paper so any insects can be easily removed. Avoid washing them if you can, and store in a plastic bag in the fridge for a couple of hours before using.

Edible flowers

How to grow **Spinach and Swiss Chard**

full sun or part shade

moist soil

Equipment

Spinach or Swiss chard seeds

A container
such as a windowbox

General-purpose compost

Watering can

Once you have tasted home-grown spinach and Swiss chard leaves you will want your own supply of them all year round. These crops are very easy to grow as well as being highly nutritious.

SOWING

Sow the seeds in shallow drills. Cover them over with compost and water in well. In a few weeks when the seedlings are large enough to handle, thin them out. Don't discard the thinnings – wash them and use in salads as baby leaves. To ensure bumper crops, make sure you keep the plants well watered and nourished, as the shallow containers will dry out quite quickly.

HARVESTING

In windowboxes, both spinach and Swiss chard plants should be picked while the leaves are still small, within about six weeks. Harvest the baby leaves and use them in salads. If the leaves of your crop have grown slightly larger, try stir-frying them, which will preserve their nutrients.

TROUBLESHOOTING

Spinach is prone to "bolting", which is when the plant rushes to flower and produce seed, making the leaves unusable. This usually occurs if the compost has been allowed to dry out, so it is important to keep it moist at all times. Water the plants once – or even twice – a day if necessary during warm, dry weather.

Spinach

Swiss chard

Grow Tomatoes in a Pot

Harvesting a bumper crop of juicy, home-grown tomatoes warmed by the summer sun is really satisfying. Growing this versatile vegetable can be as simple as planting up and caring for a shop-bought plant, so grab some from the garden centre and grow a supply of tomatoes all summer.

Equipment

- Tomato plant
- Terracotta container
- Crocks
- Peat-free compost
- Trowel
- Canes
- String
- Scissors
- Watering can
- Liquid tomato feed

Tomatoes *8–16 weeks until harvest*

Plant *out between late spring and early summer*

Water daily *and feed every two weeks once fruits appear*

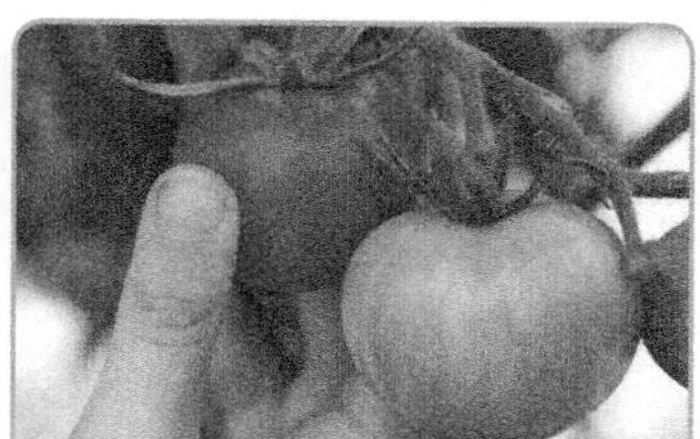

Harvest *in midsummer to mid-autumn*

1 Tomato plants are ideal for growing in containers in a sunny, sheltered location. Water the plant a couple of hours before planting, then gently remove it from its pot, being careful not to damage the roots. Part-fill your new container with peat-free general-purpose compost.

Careful! If you are growing the tomato as an upright, or "cordon" plant, avoid trailing varieties.

Take care when handling the plant to ensure the stem does not snap

Leave a small gap between the compost surface and the top of the pot

2 Place the tomato plant in the container, and fill around the root ball with compost, making sure that the base of the stem is flush with the level of the compost in the container. Gently firm the tomato plant into the compost using your fingertips.

3 Once the tomato plant is in place, it will need to be supported, as once the fruits develop it will become quite top-heavy – a bamboo cane is the simplest method (see p.77). Push the cane into the soil, making sure that you don't drive it through the plant's root system, and tie the plant to it with twine. Water the plant every day and give it a weekly feed with tomato fertilizer.

Leave a 10-cm (4-in) gap between the plant and the cane

4 The tomato plant will need to be tied in regularly as it grows, using a figure-of-eight knot to avoid damaging the stem (see p.34). Encourage fruiting by pinching out sideshoots growing from the leaf joints (see p.35). Pick the tomatoes when they turn red and are slightly soft.

Tip Towards the end of the season they can be picked green and left to ripen on a windowsill.

Caring for your **Tomatoes**

Tomatoes are the quintessential Mediterranean fruit and thrive in sunny spots, but will need regular watering to prevent them from drying out.

Things to watch out for...

Whitefly These pests can swarm a plant, sucking sap from the underside of the leaves and causing mould to form. If they become a serious problem you may want to consider using insecticide. Plant marigolds near the tomatoes as they may help to ward off whiteflies.

Potassium deficiency If the leaves turn brown and blotchy and there aren't many tomatoes on your plant, it may be short of potassium. Feed the plants once a week with a tomato fertilizer that is high in potassium, which gives the tomatoes flavour and colour. Keep plants well watered to boost their general level of health (see p.66).

Tomato blight If the leaves, stems, and tomatoes start to look brown and diseased, and then begin to rot, remove the plant immediately and destroy it.

Don't forget to support the cordon with a stake, otherwise it will snap

Pick tomatoes when slightly soft and allow them to fully ripen indoors

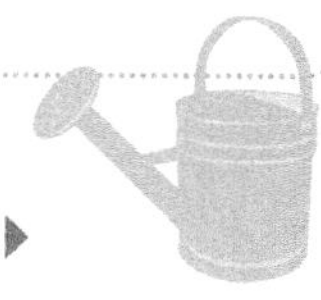

Also learn to grow ▸▸▸

How to grow **Herbs in a Pot**

full sun **light soil**

Equipment

- Chive or basil plants
- Pot of any size or shape, with drainage holes
- Crocks
- Good-quality potting compost
- Watering can

As well as being an attractive addition to the garden, chives and basil are delicious ingredients for use in a variety of dishes. Keep the plants well watered, and give them a sheltered, sunny site.

PLANTING

Before you plant the herbs in their new container, water them thoroughly an hour before planting. Turn over each pot and ease out the plant. If the plant is large and you want to divide it, hold the plant at its base, gently prise apart the root ball, and separate it into smaller clumps.

Place crocks in the base of your new container and then cover them with a layer of good-quality compost. Arrange your herb plants in the pot to your own design, making sure that there is an even coverage and that there are plants around its edge. Leave about 10cm (4in) between plants. Fill in the gaps in the compost and firm around the plants. Leave a gap of 2.5cm (1in) between the top of the compost and the pot's rim. Water well and place the pot in a sunny spot.

Tip This method can be used on any number of herb plants, so feel free to experiment depending on the herbs you like to cook with.

Chives

Basil

How to grow **Roots in a Pot**

full sun **light soil**

Equipment

- Radish or beetroot seeds
- Pot of any size or shape, with drainage holes
- Crocks
- Good-quality potting compost
- Watering can

Radishes and baby beets are ideal crops to grow for quick results. You will be picking these nutritious, tasty roots about four to five weeks after sowing. As soon as one crop is done, sow another.

SOWING

Fill your pot with compost to within 2.5cm (1in) of the rim and water well. Scatter the seeds lightly on the surface and lightly cover them with compost. Water the seeds in well. Put the pot in a sunny position and remember to keep it well watered.

GROWING

When the seedlings appear you may need to thin them to give them space to swell in size. Beet seedlings need to be about 5cm (2in) apart, and radishes 2.5cm (1in). Don't discard any seedlings, but wash and add to salads.

HARVESTING

Begin harvesting as soon as your crops reach an edible size. After about four to five weeks your baby beets and your radishes should be 2.5cm (1in) in size; don't leave them in the pot for too long, or they will turn dry and pithy. Remember to harvest baby beet leaves as well as their roots.

Tip Radishes will tolerate shade and can be planted between taller plants, such as lettuces.

Radishes

Baby beets

Grow Herbs in a Basket

Create a basket of aromas just outside your kitchen window with this beautiful display of herbs. Easy to grow no matter how small your space, this selection of herbs can be adapted to suit your culinary tastes.

full sun **light soil**

Equipment

Hanging basket with plastic liner
General-purpose compost
Horticultural grit
Herb plants
such as rosemary, chives, sage, marjoram, thyme, and lemon verbena
Trowel
Watering can
Wall bracket
Drill and screws

Hanging basket

General-purpose compost

Horticultural grit

Screws

Trowel

Watering can

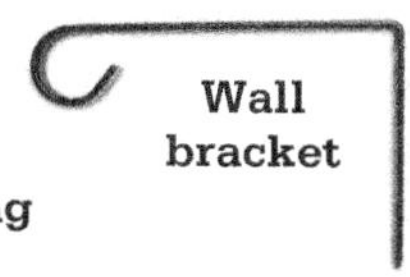
Wall bracket

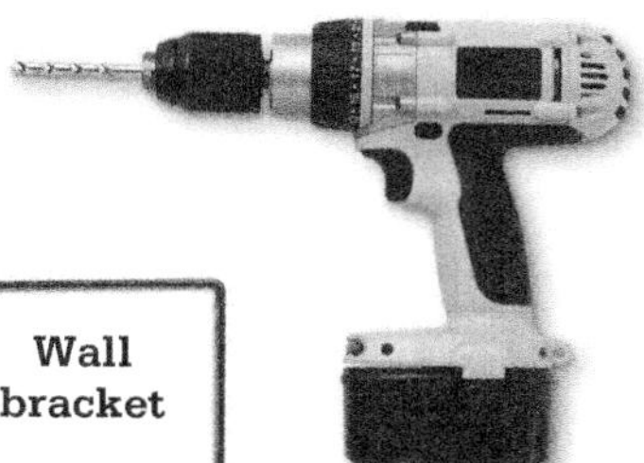
Drill

Herb plants

Herbs *4–16 weeks until harvest*

Plant out *your herbs between mid-spring and midsummer*

Water *young plants well, especially in hot summer weather*

Harvest *crops all year round, as you require them*

1 If the basket is not lined, line it with a purpose-made liner or plastic sheeting. Herbs grow best in well-drained conditions, so mix general-purpose compost with grit at a ratio of 5:1 and place this in the bottom of the basket.

Careful! Make sure the liner has drainage holes. If not, it will need piercing with a knife or scissors.

2 Choose plants that you enjoy cooking with. Plant the more upright herbs in the centre with the trailing varieties on the outside. You could also add trailing flowers such as lobelias or petunias.

Tip Avoid mint, as it is invasive and will swamp other plants.

3 There should be room for about five to six plants in an average-sized hanging basket. Place the herbs in the basket, and pack the compost and grit around the root balls, firming in with your fingertips.

Tip Only fill the basket up to 2.5cm (1in) below the basket rim, to allow space for it to be watered without overflowing.

4 Water the herbs thoroughly after planting. Hang the basket from a sturdy bracket in a warm, sheltered site. Water the plants at least once a day during summer and give them a liquid feed every week. In winter, only water if the soil is completely dry.

Tip Water in the morning or evening when the temperature is coolest so plants can absorb water before it evaporates.

Use a rose at the end of the watering can to gently distribute the water

Caring for your **Herbs**

Hanging baskets filled with herbs make the best use of a small growing space, and will only need some simple care to keep the plants healthy and happy.

Things to watch out for...

Wilted leaves Hanging baskets filled with free-draining soil will dry out very quickly, and you may find that you need to water the plants most days during the summer. Check the drainage holes so that the herbs don't sit in very damp conditions.

Powdery coating on leaves and stems Mildew creates a whitish layer on the herb foliage and may cause the leaves to become distorted in shape. Remove all infected plant material and ensure that the plants are getting enough sunshine, that their soil is not overly damp, and thin out some of the plants so that there is a good airflow around them.

New growth Regularly harvest the leaves and shoots to encourage new growth. Some herbs, such as rosemary, will benefit from a light trim in spring.

Cramped conditions The herbs in this selection are perennial and should keep going for a few years. However, because of the restricted growing conditions some of them will benefit from being divided in autumn, and potted up into a new hanging basket with fresh compost and grit.

For a vibrant display choose herbs that provide a contrast of colours and textures

Grow Onions from Sets

If you love cooking, onions are surely a must for your kitchen garden. Although they can be grown from seed, it is far easier to plant onion sets, which are basically mini-onions and can be planted straight into the ground in autumn or spring.

Equipment

- Onion sets
- Fork
- Rake
- Bamboo canes
- String
- Watering can
- Hoe
- Plant labels

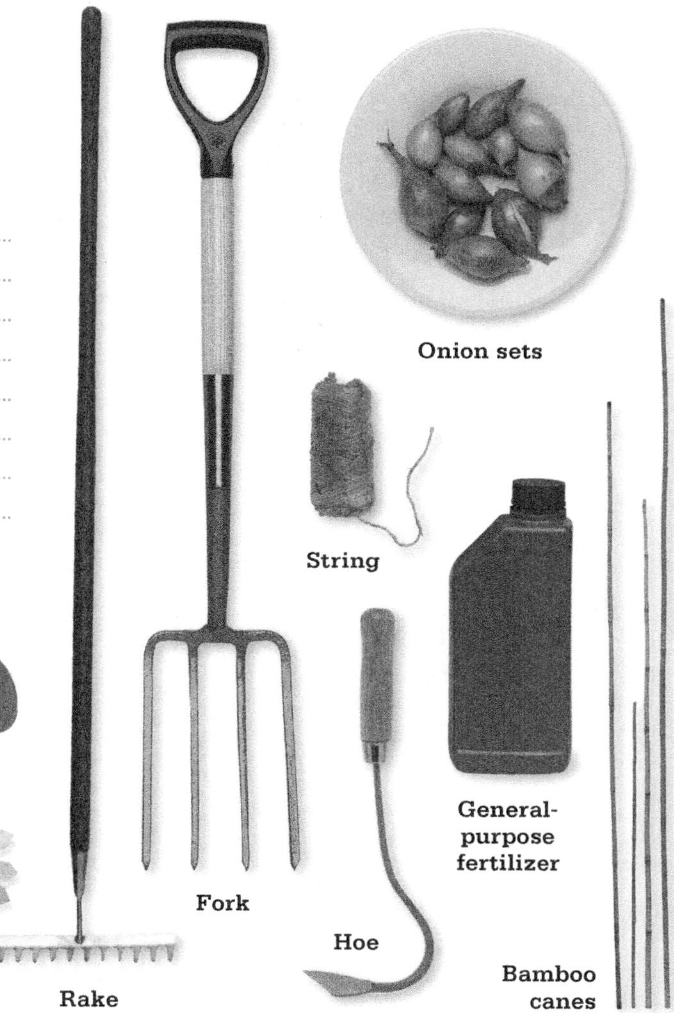

Onions *20–24 weeks until harvest*

Plant out sets *in autumn or early to mid-spring*

Weed *carefully around the seedlings as they develop*

Harvest *onions between early summer and mid-autumn*

1 In a sunny location, mark out drills 30cm (12in) apart with string (see p.72). Create a ridge in the soil using a hoe and push the onion sets into the soil leaving just the tip of each one showing above the soil. Space them 8–10cm (3–4in) apart.

Careful! Avoid planting the sets into freshly manured soil, as this can cause them to rot.

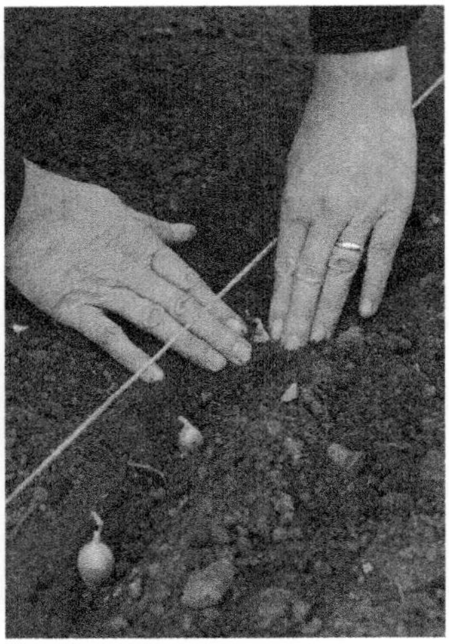

Be careful not to damage your young plants as you weed around them

2 As the sets grow you'll need to make sure you keep them free from weeds, which will compete with your crops for nutrients, water, and light. Weed along the rows by hand to avoid damaging your seedlings. Apply general-purpose fertilizer.

Tip Once the plants are larger and less vulnerable you may want to weed around them using an onion hoe instead, to save time.

3 The plants will need regular watering as they start to grow. During very dry weather, water them every day. However, take care not to overwater – ensure that the water soaks into the soil rather than sitting on the surface – as onions are prone to rotting.

Careful! Birds can pull up young seedlings, so cover them with a net if you need to (see pp.128–129).

Use a rose on your watering can to sprinkle water gently over your plants

Harvest your crop when the weather is dry to prevent them rotting

4 Most onions will be ready to harvest in late summer, when the leaves wilt and turn yellow. After harvesting, leave the onions to dry in the sun for a few days – on a rack is ideal, so that the air and warmth can surround them.

Tip Onions can be stored indoors in a cool, dry location, such as a garage, until you want to use them. Tie the stalks together to form a plait and hang them up.

Caring for your **Onions**

Grown from sets, onions are one of the easiest kitchen garden vegetables and with a little care and attention you can be harvesting your own bumper crop in no time.

Remove the dirt and soil before storing onions

Leave onions to dry before storing

Things to watch out for...

Rotting bulbs A waterlogged soil can cause onions to rot, but another cause could be onion fly. This pest tunnels into the base of the plant, rotting the bulb and eventually causing the plant to collapse. There is no cure once the pest sets in, you will have to dig up all your bulbs and destroy them. Cover young plants with fleece to help deter the pest from laying eggs nearby.

Rustling skins You'll know that your onions have been drying long enough and are ready to store once their skins become papery and start to rustle. Clean them thoroughly before you store them, so that they will keep as long as possible.

Grow Garlic

A wonderfully versatile vegetable for the kitchen, garlic is easy to grow and ideal if you don't have much space, as it will thrive in pots or windowboxes. Simply push the cloves into the soil and watch them grow.

full sun

light soil

Equipment

Garlic cloves
certified disease-free

Fork

Rake

Bamboo canes

String

Dibber

Watering can

General-purpose fertilizer

Trowel

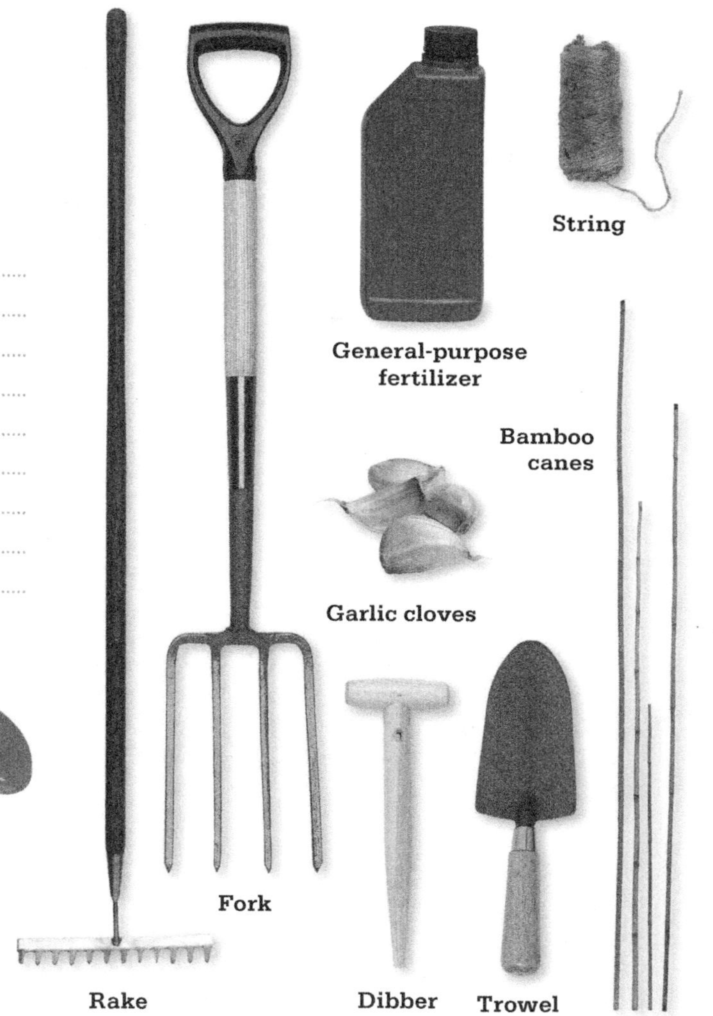

Garlic *20–36 weeks until harvest*

Plant cloves *in the ground between autumn and spring*

Weed and water *the seedlings well during summer*

Harvest *the bulbs between summer and mid-autumn*

1 Choose garlic cloves that are certified disease-free. Don't use cloves from supermarkets. They may germinate, but some will be varieties from hotter climates and may be unsuitable for cooler conditions. Pull apart the bulbs into individual cloves.

Tip They can be planted any time between autumn and spring, but cloves planted in autumn usually result in bigger crops.

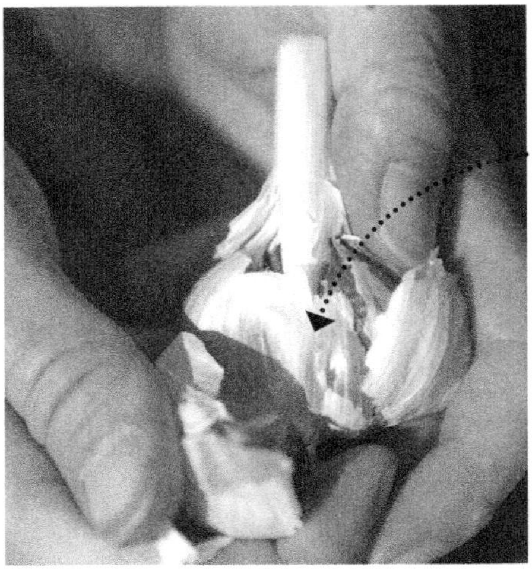

Break off individual cloves for planting and discard the stem

Use a dibber to make the hole

2 Don't manure the soil before planting as this can rot the bulb. Dig in a general-purpose fertilizer before planting. Plant the cloves in a sunny spot, with the pointed end facing upwards and poking slightly out of the ground. Space the cloves 10cm (4in) apart in rows, with a gap of 25cm (10in) between the rows. After planting, water the cloves well.

3 As the cloves grow, keep the area well weeded to prevent other plants competing with the garlic's shallow roots. Weeds can drastically reduce the yield and size of bulb.

Careful! Water during dry spells in summer, but avoid excess watering as the bulb swells, as this can cause the garlic to rot.

Bulbs can be gently lifted with a trowel

4 You can tell that the bulb is ready to harvest when the stems start to turn yellow and fold over. Carefully lift the bulbs taking care not to bruise or damage them. Leave them to dry in the sun for a few days before taking them inside to store in a cool, dry place.

Caring for your **Garlic**

Garlic is easy to grow as you don't need to sow seeds. Simply push cloves into the ground and leave them to swell – just be careful not to overwater them.

Things to watch out for...

Garden thieves You may need to protect the cloves after planting as birds are prone to pull them up – construct some secure netting to keep the pests at bay (see pp.128–129).

Orange blisters A common disease that affects garlic is leek rust, which causes orange, spore-filled blisters on the foliage. There is no cure for this disease, so dig up the plants, destroy them, and ensure that you rotate your crops the following year (see pp.134–135).

After harvesting, garlic can be plaited, as shown here, or stored in a net or a pair of old tights

If stored in a cool dry place, the bulbs should last for a few months

Avoid hanging the plait in the kitchen unless you plan on using cloves quickly

Grow Strawberries in a Basket

A hanging basket dripping with glistening red berries is a lovely sight. If you want to enjoy home-grown strawberries with cream throughout the summer, plant up a basket of these delicious fruits.

full sun

light soil

Equipment

- Hanging basket with plastic liner
- General-purpose compost
- Controlled-release fertilizer
- Trowel
- 3 strawberry plants
- Watering can
- Wall bracket
- Drill and screws

Hanging basket

General-purpose compost

Screws

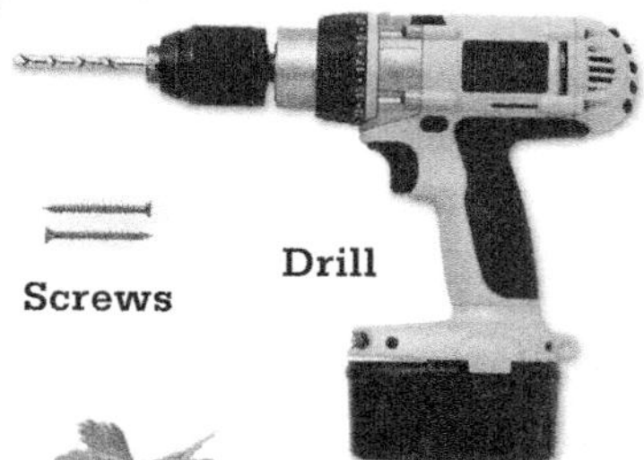

Drill

Watering can

Wall bracket

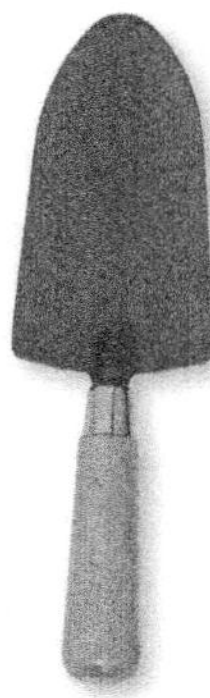

Trowel

Strawberry plants

Controlled-release fertilizer

Strawberries *4–6 weeks until harvest*

Plant out *in early to mid-spring once frosts have passed*

Water *the growing plants well during the summer*

Harvest *between late spring and mid-autumn*

Use scissors to cut several holes in the sides and base of the liner

1 Choose a large hanging basket with a liner. If the liner does not already have drainage holes, cut them yourself to allow the soil to drain, which will prevent the strawberry plants from rotting.

Careful! Ensure you have a sturdy place such as a fence post or wall to hang your basket as it will be very heavy when filled.

2 Fill the hanging basket with some good-quality general-purpose compost and add a slow- or controlled-release fertilizer to keep the plants well supplied with nutrients as they grow.

Tip If the basket has a rounded bottom, stand it in a large plant pot to keep it secure as you fill it.

Mix the controlled-release fertilizer with the compost

Fill about two-thirds full of compost to leave room for the plants

3 Plant three strawberry plants so that just the crowns of the plants, the points at which all the stems sprout from, are above the surface of the compost. Firm the plants in gently, using your fingertips.

Tip Choose one seedling each of early, mid, and late varieties and you'll have fruit for a longer period.

4 Strawberry plants can produce fruit for more than one year if you want them to. To keep them going, reduce the crop in the first year by removing some of the flowers. When pinching out, snap the flowers off at the base of the stem, taking care not to damage the plant.

Tip Some strawberries produce pink flowers, which make an attractive alternative for display.

5 Water the plant thoroughly after planting, then hang in a sunny, sheltered spot. Water the plants every day during the growing season.

Careful! If the leaves start to turn yellow, give the plants a feed with liquid tomato fertilizer.

Caring for your **Strawberries**

Strawberries are very easy to grow and perfect for a beginner to try, just ensure that you keep them well fed and watered and keep birds at bay.

Fruit will last longer if you include 2cm (¾in) of stalk when you pick it

Pick strawberries regularly when they turn bright red to keep the plant cropping

Things to watch out for...

Dry soil During the summer, strawberry plants need regular watering and their soil should not be allowed to dry out. Ideally you should also give them a balanced liquid feed once a week.

Garden thieves As the fruit starts to ripen it will become irresistible to pests such as birds and wasps. Place a net over the basket to keep birds out and hang a jam trap – a jam jar with some jam and water in the bottom – nearby to deter wasps.

The angle of the sun If you can, turn the hanging basket every few days to ensure that light reaches all parts of the plants. This will encourage the fruit to swell and ripen.

Old foliage To keep the plants fruiting for the following year, cut back the old foliage after harvesting, leaving just new, young leaves.

Also learn to grow ▸▸▸

How to grow **Tumbling Tomatoes**

full sun

light soil

Equipment

3 trailing tomato plants

Hanging basket with good drainage

General-purpose compost

Controlled-release fertilizer

Watering can

TRAILING TOMATOES

Trailing, or tumbling, tomatoes are a wonderful savoury alternative to strawberries for a hanging basket and are just as easy to grow. Growing them in hanging baskets keeps them away from slugs and allows you to pick the fruit comfortably. Position the basket close to the kitchen for convenience.

PLANTING

Part-fill the hanging basket with good-quality compost and mix in controlled-release fertilizer at the recommended rate. Arrange three trailing tomatoes around the edge of the basket, fill around them with soil, firm in, and water well.

Keep the plants well watered and feed regularly with tomato fertilizer. The plants will tumble gracefully down as they grow. Pick the tomatoes as they ripen, depending on the variety this could be within as little as a few months. Tomatoes are annual plants so remove the plants after cropping and add to the compost heap.

RIPENING

If you want to speed up the ripening process while the tomatoes are still growing outside, you can place banana skins on the surface of the compost in the hanging basket. A chemical naturally produced by these fruits will rapidly colour up your tomatoes.

Harvest all remaining tomatoes before the first autumn frosts. Don't worry if the tomatoes are green as they will ripen on the windowsill inside. Alternatively you can make green tomato chutney.

TROUBLESHOOTING

Watch out for tomato blight, which is a fungus that spreads amongst the foliage and will quickly kill the plants. Remove foliage that is turning brown as soon as you spot it and dispose of it immediately.

How to **Carry Out Basic Plant Care**

It is important to take regular care of your plants. They will need watering, feeding, and protection from pests and diseases. Seedlings should be kept free from competing weeds. Look after your plants well and they will reward you with bumper crops to harvest later in the year.

Pests and disease

Keep an eye out for any diseased plant material and remove it as soon as you see it. Monitor leaves and crops for signs of damage from pests such as aphids and remove them before the problem spreads. Plants bred to be resistant to diseases are available, but healthy, well-fed plants will be less likely to attract pests and fall prey to diseases.

Regular watering

Keep plants well watered so that they remain strong and healthy and are able to resist disease. In warm conditions, such as greenhouses and on window ledges, emerging seedlings will need watering at least once a day. Crops in containers will need more frequent watering than those in the open ground, as pots will drain faster.

How to **Protect Plants from Slugs**

These silent, slimy pests can be devastating, as they devour almost any green foliage they come across, munching their way through the vegetable patch, particularly at night and in moist, damp conditions. Don't worry though, there are plenty of ways to deal with them.

Place grit or sand around the plants

Place slug collars around plants

Slug-proofing your plants

Placing a barrier of grit or sand around your seedlings will deter slugs because they don't like the sharp, dry texture. Slug collars, which can be bought from the garden centre, will also discourage slugs and snails, while pots filled with beer will lure slugs in and trap them. Copper tape placed around the rim of pots gives a slight static shock to slugs that try to cross it, and slug pellets are also effective. Choose the option that suits you best.

How to **Feed**

Feeding your plants regularly will keep them healthy and maximize your crop. There is a variety of feeds and fertilizers available, which should be applied to your plants at crucial stages of their growth and fruit production. It is also important to regularly replenish the nutrients the plants take from the soil by digging in well-rotted manure.

Tip Always add fertilizer to the compost when planting up containers and hanging baskets. When plants have their roots contained, they are completely dependent on being fed with fertilizers to produce fruit or vegetables.

Feeding

To boost crops, use a general fertilizer with balanced amounts of nitrogen, phosphorus, and potassium (see pp.24–25). A fertilizer high in potash will encourage a larger number of fruits on your plants, and is especially useful for "hungry" crops such as tomatoes, peppers, and brassicas, which benefit from extra feeds. Controlled-release fertilizer is expensive, but releases the required nutrients when the plant needs them throughout the year.

How to **Weed**

Don't give weeds a chance to swamp your plants, as they may block out light and will take moisture and nutrients from the soil. It is important to remove any weeds from your site before you sow or plant out, as they can reproduce prolifically and some can root deep into the soil, making them difficult to remove once crops are in place.

Make sure no perennial roots remain as these will quickly regenerate

Use a fork to dislodge larger weeds because a spade can cut the roots, causing them to multiply

Look out for small weeds that will compete with the seedlings for nutrients

Pull out weeds that are close to seedlings by hand to avoid damaging the plants

Small weeds in the ground or in containers are best removed by hand

Weeding

Even though you will have weeded your site when you prepared to plant (see p.15), you will still need to weed regularly, especially in the summer months. It is vital that annual weeds, such as groundsel, do not have a chance to set seed and that perennial weeds, such as dandelions, do not take hold. Weed between the rows using a fork or rake, taking care not to damage the plants, or for smaller rows of seedlings pull out the weeds by hand.

2

Build On It

This chapter will show you how to build on the skills and techniques you have learned so far, and extend the range of tasty culinary treats you can grow yourself.

In this section learn to grow:

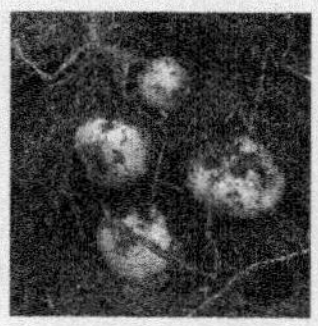

Potatoes
see pp.78–81

Courgettes
see pp.82–85

Peppers
see pp.88–92

Carrots
see pp.94–97

Cabbages
see pp.100–104

Beans
see pp.106–110

Raspberries
see pp.112–115

Apples
see pp.116–120

Currants
see pp.122–125

How to **Sow in Drills and Thin Out**

Seeds that can be sown directly into the ground are most commonly sown in drills. To create your drill, insert canes where you want it to start and end, and then tie a piece of garden twine or string between them. With the string as a guide, use a hoe to create a shallow trench between the canes – this is where you will sow your seeds.

Sowing

Thinning out

Getting your seeds started

Water the drill, then sprinkle the seeds into it, at the spacing given on the seed packet. Gently cover the seeds with soil and water in well. Once the seeds germinate and show their first true leaves, thin them out by hand, leaving the strongest to grow on. It is important to do this so that your seedlings are not competing for water, light, and nutrients. The ideal distance between them will vary for each crop, so always check the seed packet.

How to **Pot On**

Plants that were sown indoors and have begun to outgrow their pots but can't be moved outdoors because conditions are still too cold, will need to be "potted on" – put into a new, larger pot to maintain healthy growth. Make sure you use fresh compost recommended for seed sowing.

Gently squeeze the pot to loosen the compost, making it easy to remove your seedling

Look at the root system to see if there is room for the plant to grow

Re-potting seedlings

Hold the seedling gently by its first leaves, never by its stem

Use a pencil or a dibber to tease the seedling's roots from the compost

Separating seedlings

Dividing and potting on

Seedlings are ready to be potted on when their roots begin to fill their pots and when their first leaves have expanded and new leaves are beginning to develop between them. Part-fill your new, larger pot with fresh compost and give it a good water. Gently remove your seedling from its pot and replant it. Seedlings grown in seed trays will also need separating and planting on – gently pull them apart and replant in individual pots.

How to **Harden Off and Protect from Frost**

Cold temperatures can cause your crops to shrivel and die so it's important to both prepare and protect them. Plants that have been grown indoors and have tender leaves will need to be hardened off before they are planted outside otherwise they may be damaged by frosts or strong winds.

Harden off outside

Harden off on the porch

Hardening off

To prepare your crops for cooler outdoor temperatures, place them outside during the day and bring them inside at night for two weeks. Alternatively, place them in a cold frame for a few days or even just on the porch if no frosts are forecast. This will allow the plants to adjust and slowly acclimatize to the temperature. After this they will be ready to plant out but may still need further protection, so keep an eye on the forecast.

Homemade cloches

Crops that have been planted out may still need protection from the weather if frosts are threatened. Cloches prevent plants from being damaged by cold weather as they act as a miniature greenhouse, trapping warm air around the plant, with the added bonus of also protecting them against pests. Cut away the bases of see-through plastic bottles to make your own.

Shop-bought cloches

Seeds that have been sown outside will need protection from cold weather, and a shop-bought glass or polythene cloche can do just that. Large cloches like this can also be used to warm up the soil before seeds are sown, to ensure your crops have the best possible start. Simply place the cloche in position a few weeks before you plan to sow.

Cold frames

Whether you buy one or make one, cold frames look attractive in the garden and provide protection to vegetables that are in pots or containers. The low wooden structures have a transparent lid of glass or plastic and give plants protection from the cold, while also allowing them essential light.

How to **Mulch**

Mulching involves covering the soil around your plants with a generous layer of material such as manure, compost, or bark chips to suppress weeds, retain moisture, and improve the soil quality. Straw can also be used as a mulch to lift strawberries off the soil and keep plants well ventilated.

Straw

Bark chippings

Compost

Well-rotted manure

Mulching

Outdoor plants should be mulched in springtime, after planting and watering. Biodegradable mulches such as compost, manure, or leaf mould, break down to release nutrients into the soil and help it to retain moisture. Be careful to keep compost off the foliage though, as it will damage it. Non-biodegradable mulches such as pebbles or stone chippings are often used and can make a decorative addition to the garden.

How to **Stake**

Supporting crops with bamboo canes or wooden stakes will prevent tall or top-heavy plants, such as brassicas, or those that are heavily burdened with fruit or vegetables, such as peppers or tomatoes, from collapsing, which would risk the health of the plant and its crop.

Careful positioning

Tying the cane

Staking

Insert your bamboo cane or wooden stake into the ground so that it is close to the main stem of your plant, but be careful not to damage the roots as you do so. Ensure that it is secure and vertical. Using garden twine or string, tie your plants to their stakes using figure-of-eight knots (see p.34). Keep an eye on the plants as they develop and add more supports if you need to. Some plants, such as runner beans, will require staking from a very early stage.

Grow Potatoes in a Tub

Potatoes are the staple vegetable for many aspiring kitchen gardeners. Not only are they easy to grow, but planting tubers in large containers is also a simple way to produce a bumper crop even if you don't have much space.

full sun

moist soil

Equipment

- Potato tubers
- Egg box
- Deep container
  such a large tub, with drainage holes
- Crocks
- General-purpose compost
- Trowel
- Watering can

Crocks

General-purpose compost

Trowel

Potato tubers

Watering can

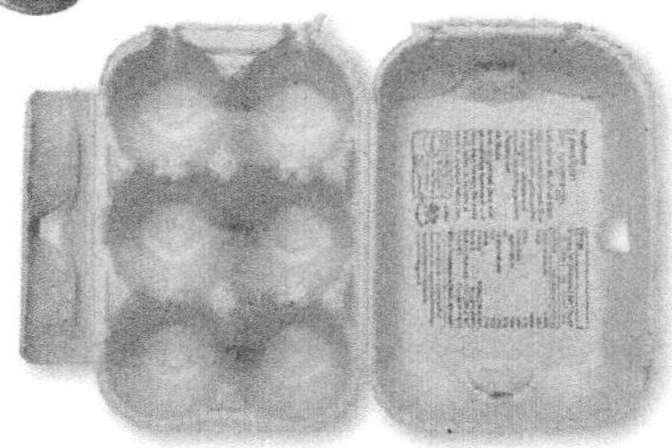

Egg box

Deep container

Potatoes *12–22 weeks until harvest*

Chit potatoes *in a cool place in early to mid-spring*

Plant out *your potatoes in early to mid-spring*

Earth up *the growing plants during summer*

Harvest *during summer and into autumn*

1 Most potatoes benefit from being chitted in early spring. Chitting is the process of sprouting the potatoes before planting. Put potato tubers in an egg box, with the end with the most sprouts or "eyes", facing upwards. Place the box on a window ledge to sprout the shoots.

Tip The potatoes are ready to plant after a few weeks, when the shoots are about 2cm (¾in) long.

These chits will get the potatoes growing quickly once placed in the soil

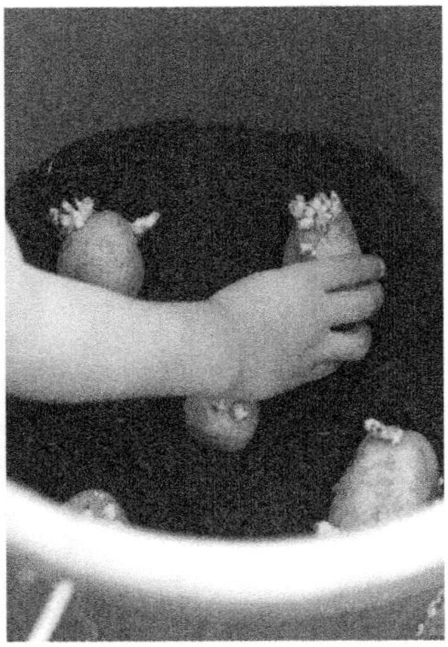

2 Choose a large container or a plastic bin with drainage holes – if it doesn't have any you'll need to create some yourself – and fill it one-third full with general-purpose compost. Evenly space five potatoes in the container. Cover the potatoes with compost so the container is now two-thirds full.

Tip Main crop potatoes can be grown in tubs if you just plant two or three tubers instead of five.

3 Place the container in a sunny, sheltered location. The potatoes will need to be "earthed up" as they grow. This means packing compost around the plants, leaving the top few leaves uncovered, until it reaches the top of the container.

Why? Earthing up prevents light reaching the tubers – this stops them turning green and inedible, and increases the yield.

Make sure that the tubers are not exposed to sunlight until they are ready to harvest

4 Keep the plants well watered as they grow and make sure they are not allowed to dry out. Potatoes will be ready to harvest just as they finish flowering; dig one up to check if it is ready. To harvest, tip the container upside down and pick out the potatoes.

Tip Harvest on a dry day, and leave the tubers out in the sunshine for a few hours.

Caring for your **Potatoes**

Growing potatoes in a tub makes them much less susceptible to pests and diseases than those grown in the ground – just don't let the tubers see the light.

Things to watch out for...

Dying flowers Once your flowers start to die it is time to harvest. Early potatoes are best eaten immediately but main crops and salad potatoes can be stored for longer in a cool, dark place. See p.185 for details on storage.

Green tubers If the potatoes are exposed to daylight they become green and inedible and should not be eaten. Take care to earth up plants deeply to avoid this.

Patchy, rotten foliage Potato blight is a fungus that causes the leaves of potato plants to rot, before spreading to the tubers. Remove and destroy any infected foliage, and choose resistant varieties in future years.

Take care not to pierce your potatoes when harvesting with a fork

Grow Courgettes in a Bag

Courgettes are very easy plants to grow if you provide them with the conditions they need – give them plenty of sun, water, and an abundance of compost and you will be harvesting crops all summer long. Growing them in a planting bag is ideal if your garden space is limited.

full sun **moist soil**

Equipment

- Courgette seeds
- Small plastic pots
- General-purpose compost
- Dibber
- Planting bag
- Crocks
- Trowel
- Gloves
- Watering can
- Liquid fertilizer

Small plastic pots

General-purpose compost

Trowel

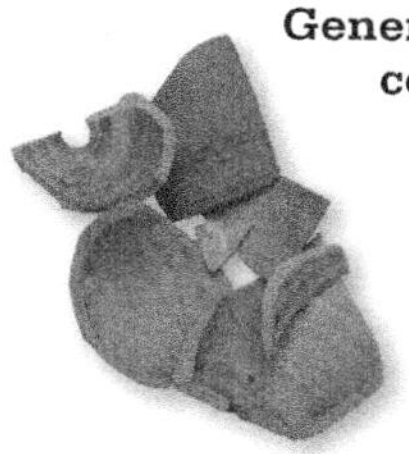

Crocks

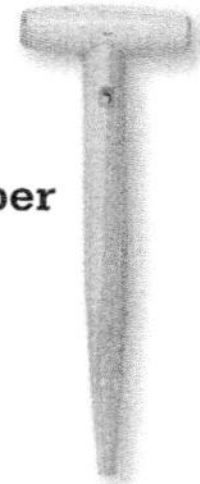

Dibber

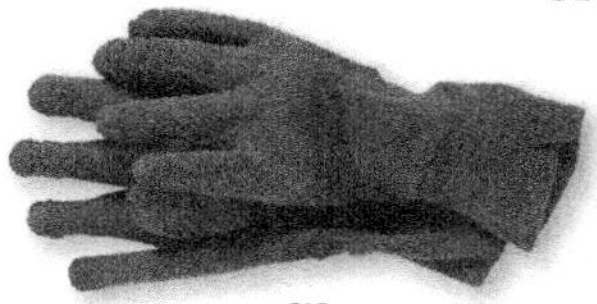

Gloves

Watering can

Liquid fertilizer

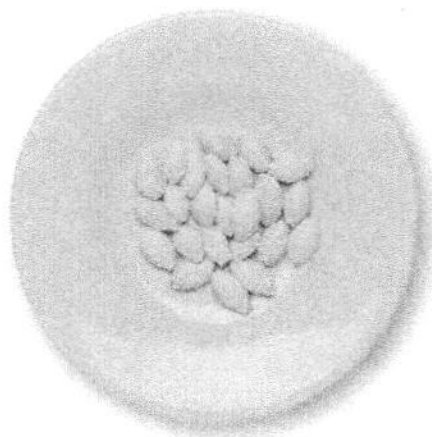

Courgette seeds

Planting bag

Courgettes *14 weeks until harvest*

Sow your seeds *in mid-spring under cover*

Harden off *in late spring to early summer*

Water *the growing plants throughout summer*

Harvest *from midsummer to mid-autumn*

1 Courgette seeds should be sown in mid-spring. Fill small plastic pots with general-purpose compost. Use a dibber to create a hole and sow one seed per pot, 2.5cm (1in) deep. Place on a sunny windowsill to germinate.

Tip Place the seed on its side to stop it from rotting in the pot – water can run off it rather than collect on its wide surface.

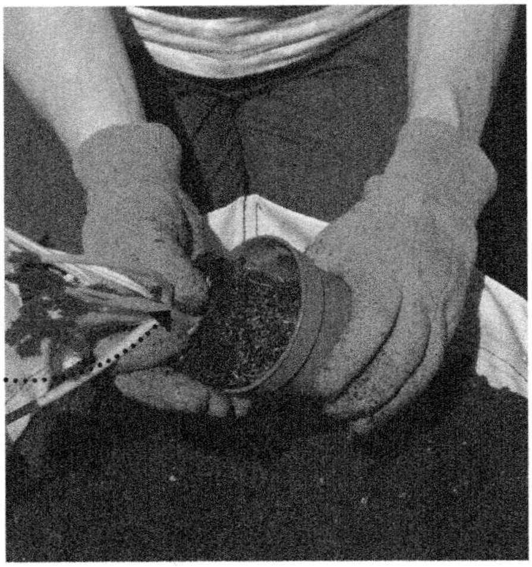

Be careful not to damage the stem

2 Once the risk of frost is over in late spring or early summer, harden the plants off (see p.74). Create holes in the bottom of the planting bag, move it into a sunny, sheltered spot, and then fill it with good-quality general purpose compost, leaving a gap of about 10cm (4in) at the top. Water the courgette well and then ease it out of its pot gently, being careful not to damage the roots.

3 Make a small hole in the middle of the planting bag and plant the courgette so that the base of the plant is level with the top of the compost. Firm the plant in well using your fingers.

Tip If you mix the compost with well-rotted manure, you will give a further boost to the hungry plant.

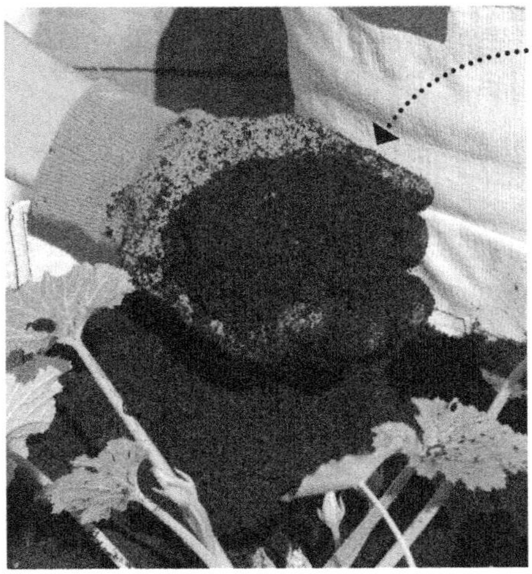

Wear gloves when handling compost, manure, or fertilizers

4 Water the plant in well. Courgettes are hungry plants and will need feeding with a liquid feed every couple of weeks.

Careful! Once the courgettes are ready to harvest, pick regularly; if courgettes are left on the plant, they will swell up to the size of marrows and the plant will stop producing other fruits.

Avoid watering at midday as this can scorch the leaves

Caring for your **Courgettes**

Courgettes are heavy croppers, virtually trouble-free, and incredibly versatile – they can be grown in bags, directly in the soil, or even on top of a compost heap.

Turn the bags regularly to ensure all the courgettes receive sunlight

Courgettes are annual plants, so remove them after they have finished cropping and add to the compost heap

Things to watch out for...

Colourful blooms Beautiful courgette flowers taste delicious fried up as fritters. Harvest a few while the plant is growing, but don't remove them all, or you won't get any courgettes. They can be stored in the fridge in a sealed bag for a few days.

Greyish, mouldy leaves Courgettes are generally disease-free but they can suffer from mildew if their roots get dry; this causes mould to form on the upper surfaces of the leaves. Remove any infected leaves and water the plants well. As the plants here are grown in bags, they will be prone to dry out quicker than if they were in the ground.

Also learn to grow ▸▸▸

How to grow **Pumpkins and Marrows**

full sun **moist soil**

Equipment

- Pumpkin or marrow seeds
- 10-cm (4-in) plastic pots
- Spade
- Well-rotted manure or compost
- Trowel
- Watering can

These large vegetables need lots of time to grow so they will not be ready until late in the season – just in time for autumn and winter feasts.

LOCATION

Both crops need full sun and a rich, fertile soil. Pumpkins can be trained up fences or walls; marrows will grow in containers or growing bags.

SOWING

In your pots, sow individual seeds on their sides to discourage decay and cover them up with compost. When the risk of frosts is over, plant out the seedlings at a distance of 1.5m (5ft) for pumpkins and 1m (3ft) for marrows. Keep them well watered.

To grow a larger pumpkin, choose a large variety and remove all flowers except one per plant. A liquid feed each week will encourage good growth.

HARVESTING

Pumpkins and marrows should be left on the vine for as long as possible to allow the skins to harden. This will prevent them from rotting in storage. Harvest when the fruits are large and swollen and leave the pumpkins in a sunny spot to ripen further. Both can be stored in a cool, well-ventilated area for around six months.

Pumpkin

Marrow

How to grow **Winter and Summer Squashes**

full sun **moist soil**

Equipment

- Winter or summer squash seeds
- Spade or trowel
- Well-rotted manure or compost
- Watering can
- Cloche

Both winter and summer squashes come in a wide range of shapes, sizes, and colours, and can liven up any vegetable patch.

SOWING

Sow winter squash seeds directly into rich, fertile soil in late spring. Sow pairs of seeds 3cm ($1^1/_4$in) deep and 1m (3ft) apart. Use a bottle cloche to cover them. Keep them well watered.

Summer squash seeds are sown directly into the soil, 45cm (18in) apart, after the risk of frost has passed. These thirsty plants will need almost constant watering as they grow.

GROWING

These trailing plants can be trained up canes or trellis. Winter squashes are ideal for growing on the ground among taller plants such as sweetcorn, and for smothering out weeds.

HARVESTING

Summer squashes will be ready to harvest from midsummer; winter squashes in late autumn to winter. Summer squashes can be harvested early when they are small or left to grow larger for roasting or stuffing. The longer you leave a summer squash on the vine, the thicker its skin will become and the longer it will store. Winter squashes store well in a cool, well-ventilated place.

Winter squash

Summer squash

Grow Peppers in a Pot

In colours ranging from purple and yellow to green, one or two pepper plants can provide enough fruit for a family throughout the summer. They are ideal for containers and hardly take up any space, so try growing these mild- or spicy-flavoured crunchy fruits for yourself.

full sun **moist soil**

Equipment

- Pepper seeds
- Plastic pots, small and large
- General-purpose compost
- Trowel
- Propagator
- Canes
- String
- Watering can
- Secateurs
- Gloves
- High-potash liquid feed

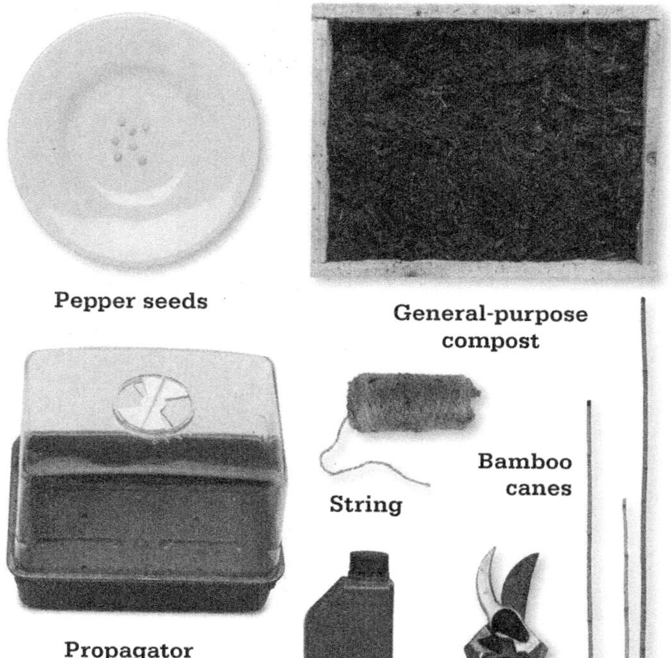

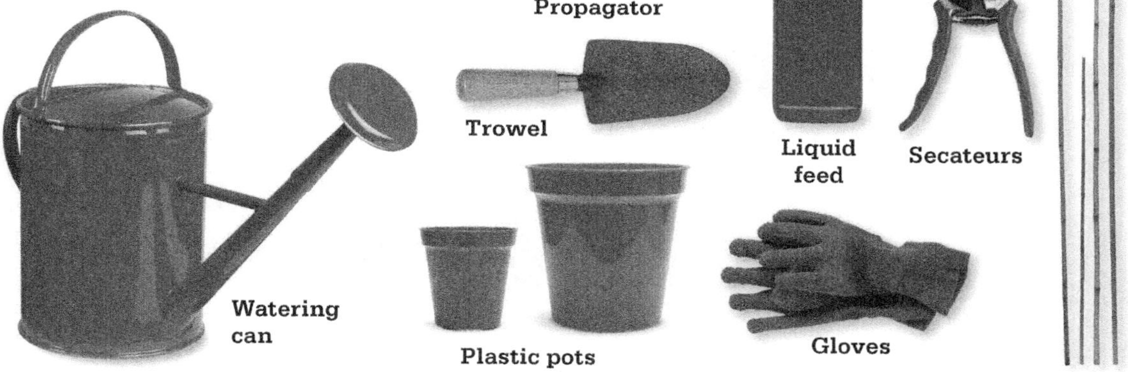

Peppers *20–26 weeks until harvest*

Sow *seed in early to mid-spring and place in a propagator*

Plant out *in early summer, after the frosts have passed*

Water *the growing plants well as they develop peppers*

Harvest *in summer through to the end of autumn*

1 Pepper plants are tender and require a long growing season, so sow them indoors in early spring to give them a good start. Sow seeds individually in small plastic pots filled with general-purpose compost. Cover the seeds over with a thin layer of compost and place the pots in a heated propagator set to around 20–24°C (68–75°F) for a week or two.

Sow only one seed in each pot

Gently remove the plant from its pot, being careful not to damage the roots

Check to see if there is a healthy root system

2 Peppers are ready to be potted on when their roots start showing through the holes in the bottom of the pot. Select some of the strongest seedlings, bearing in mind that you will only need about two or three plants for the year, and pot them up into 9-cm (3½-in) plastic pots.

Tip Give the plants a feed with a high-potash tomato fertilizer.

3 When the seedlings reach about 20cm (8in) tall, they should again be potted on into larger pots to give the plants more space to grow. It is important for the plants to get as strong and healthy as possible before being transferred outside.

Tip Pinch out the plants when they reach 20cm (8in) tall, to encourage them to branch out.

Make sure to water the plant well to keep it growing strong

These flowers will eventually develop into peppers

4 Peppers can be grown in a greenhouse, but if they are to be planted outside you will need to harden the plants off by leaving them outdoors during the day and bringing them in at night for a couple of weeks (see p.74). Once the plants have been hardened off, they can be planted into growing bags, containers, or directly into the soil at a spacing of 40cm (15in).

5 As the plants grow they will need staking. Insert a stout bamboo cane into each pot near the base of the plant, being careful not to damage the roots. Tie the plant to it using garden twine in a figure-of-eight knot (see p.34). When the first fruits appear, start feeding the plants with a high-potash liquid feed each week.

Make sure the stake is firmly "planted" in the pot

Keep tying the plant to the stake as it grows

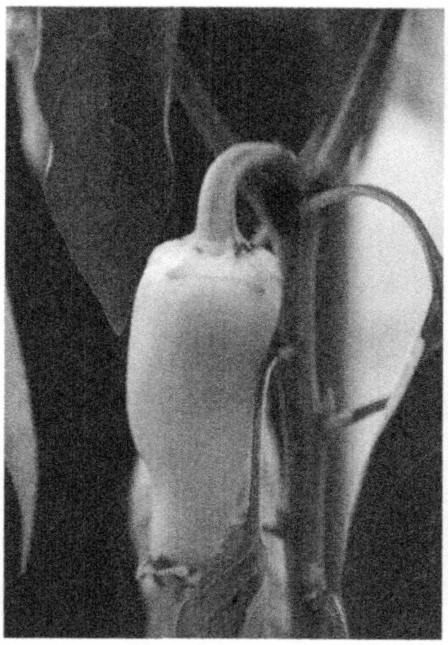

6 When fruits start ripening they will first turn green and then red, yellow, purple, or orange, depending on the variety chosen. Use a sharp pair of secateurs to remove them from the plants.

Tip It is important to harvest them promptly so that the plant can devote its energy to ripening the remaining peppers.

Caring for your **Peppers**

These tender plants need to get off to an early start as they require a long ripening period. Feed them regularly and stake them, to keep them strong and healthy.

If the leaves are looking yellow, give the plants a high-potash liquid feed

Fruits will change from green to red or yellow as they ripen

Throw a cloche over the plant if fruits haven't ripened before autumn

Things to watch out for...

Indoor plants If you are growing peppers indoors, they will need to be pollinated by hand, as flying insects won't be able to access the flowers to cross-pollinate them. Stroke the insides of the flowers with a small paintbrush to pass the pollen from one flower to another. If you are growing in a greenhouse, remember to open vents and doors on hot days to keep plants well ventilated, and damp down the door – wet it with a sponge – to keep moisture levels up.

Garden pests Although peppers are affected by few diseases, there are pests that might trouble your crops, such as aphids. These pests can swarm a plant and cover it with sticky honeydew, on which mould can grow. Apply an appropriate insecticide to control them.

Tall plants with few sideshoots The tips of the seedlings should be pinched when they are about 20cm (8in) tall. This will encourage the plant to produce more fruiting sideshoots.

Also learn to grow ▸▸▸

How to grow **Sweetcorn**

full sun | **light soil**

Equipment

- Sweetcorn seeds
- 9-cm (3½-in) plastic pots
- General-purpose compost
- Trowel
- Bamboo canes and string

SOWING

Start sweetcorn off under cover in mid-spring, sowing individual seeds into 9-cm (3½-in) pots. Keep them on a sunny windowsill or greenhouse bench. When the risk of frost is over, prepare your soil thoroughly and harden the plants off (see p.74).

Plant the sweetcorn in blocks or grids rather than single rows. They are wind-pollinated, and planting them closely in blocks ensures that pollen will pass from one plant to another, giving you high yields. Water the plants well after planting out and keep watering them regularly throughout the summer months, especially as the cobs develop.

STAKING

Stake the plants as they start to get taller using canes and string (see p.77), and earth up the bases with soil to make them more sturdy.

TROUBLESHOOTING

Keep an eye out for badgers and deer, which can devour an entire crop overnight. Cover the plants with netting to protect them from birds.

HARVESTING

To check whether the sweetcorn is ready for harvesting, peel back the green sheath and press a thumbnail into one of the kernels. If milky sap spurts out, it is ready for harvesting. Sweetcorn is an annual crop, so dig up the plants after they've cropped and add them to the compost heap.

PLANT COMBINATIONS

Grow squashes in between the taller sweetcorn plants as they will help to suppress weeds.

Grow Carrots in a Bag

This deliciously sweet and crunchy crop is a kitchen staple. The roots will need a light, well-drained soil to grow straight and smooth, and the plants will need protection from carrot fly pests. Grow them in deep containers and keep them close to the kitchen for convenience.

full sun

light soil

Equipment

- Carrot seeds
- Deep container
- General-purpose compost
- Trowel
- Bamboo canes
- Insect-proof netting
- Watering can

Carrot seeds

General-purpose compost

Insect-proof netting

Bamboo canes

Watering can

Trowel

Deep container

Carrots *12–20 weeks until harvest*

Sow *seed from mid-spring onwards after the risk of frost*

Thin *the seedlings after a few weeks in mid- to late spring*

Harvest crops *throughout summer and into autumn*

1 Ensure that your container has drainage holes and then fill it with compost. Mix in a general fertilizer and create a seed drill by pressing a piece of bamboo cane lightly across the surface, 1cm (½in) deep. If space allows, create another drill 15cm (6in) away from the first.

Tip If you do not have a piece of bamboo cane, use a biro or pencil.

2 Using all the seeds in the packet, sow thinly along the drills. Lightly brush back the soil to fill in the drill, being careful not to disturb the seeds. Water them in well using a watering can with a fine rose.

3 After a few weeks the seeds should have germinated, but they will need thinning out so that the strongest can grow to full size (see p.72). Thin to leave the plants 4cm (1½in) apart.

Careful! It is best to thin crops in the early morning or evening, when carrot fly is least active (see facing page); they are attracted to the plants' scent, which is released when their leaves are disturbed.

The thinnings from carrots can be re-planted in another bed

4 To prevent an attack by carrot fly (see below) create a barrier of fleece that, together with the container, is 60cm (24in) high; carrot fly is a low-flying pest and will not be able to fly over it and lay its eggs nearby. Alternatively, lift the container so that it is the same height off the ground.

Tip Weed around the carrots as they grow, being careful not to disturb the plants.

Caring for your **Carrots**

As long as you can protect them from carrot fly and give them a regular supply of water, carrots are easy crops to please and can be harvested in as little as 12 weeks.

Things to watch out for...

Carrot fly This pest is a persistent problem for carrots. Its larvae tunnel into the roots, making them unsightly and inedible. Thin in the early morning or evening, erect fleece guards around the plants, and choose resistant varieties such as 'Flyaway'. Alternatively, try growing strong-scented plants such as onions next to them to "mask" their scent.

Crooked roots If there are stones or clumps of hard ground in your compost carrot roots may become misshapen; they prefer light, sandy soils, which allow long roots to develop.

Unused space Carrots will be ready to harvest about 12 weeks after sowing. To make the most of your space and to give yourself a steady supply of carrots, make small sowings throughout the growing season – this will also help to ensure you don't end up with a glut.

Also learn to grow ▸▸▸

How to grow **Turnips and Beetroots**

full sun **light soil**

Equipment

- Turnip or beetroot seeds
- Module trays
- Dibber
- Trowel
- Bamboo canes and string
- Fork and rake
- Watering can

Beetroots are easy to grow and are a delicious, colourful addition to any salad. Grow turnips for their tasty roots and for their leaves, or "turnip tops".

SOWING

Sow turnip seed in modules under cover and once the risk of frost has passed, plant seedlings out in the ground 10cm (4in) apart with 30cm (12in) between rows. Keep them well watered.

The simplest way to sow beetroot is directly into the soil. Its seeds are large and easy to handle. It should be sown directly into drills 2.5cm (1in) deep and 4cm (1½in) apart. When the seedlings emerge, thin them out to 10cm (4in) apart – save the tender thinnings to use in salads.

HARVESTING

Turnips can be lifted after just five to six weeks as sweet, tender roots; when fully mature at 10 weeks they make a gourmet treat with their earthy flavours. They can also be treated as cut-and-come-again plants if you harvest the young leaves.

Harvest beetroots gently with a garden fork once they reach the size of a large orange – this will be after about 12–16 weeks. They can be stored in the same way as carrots (see p.182).

Turnips

Beetroots

How to grow **Parsnips**

full sun

light soil

Equipment

- Parsnip seeds
- Hoe and fork
- Bamboo canes and string
- Watering can
- Gloves

Parsnips are grown in much the same way as carrots and produce long, edible taproots. They take a long time to grow, but are worth the effort because they are one of the few vegetables hardy enough to stay in the ground during winter. Like carrots, their seeds don't last long, so always check the "use by" date on the packet.

SOWING

Parsnips like light, well-drained soil in full sun. The seeds should be sown directly into the soil as they don't transplant well from pots because of their long taproots. Sow the seeds from mid- to late spring once the risk of a harsh frost is over. Use bamboo canes and string to mark out rows, then create 2cm (¾in) deep drills. Sow clumps of four to five seeds every 20–30cm (8–12in). The rows should be 30cm (12in) apart.

As the seedlings emerge, thin them out leaving the strongest plant every 20–30cm (8–12in).

TROUBLESHOOTING

Look out for carrot fly, which can attack parsnips. Erect an insect-proof mesh barrier that is at least 60cm (24in) high around the plants.

HARVESTING AND STORING

It is best not to harvest your parsnips until they have been hit by the first frost, as this makes them sweeter. Lift them carefully using a fork.

Parsnips can stay in the ground for most of the winter. However, if you need to create more space for sowing early-spring vegetables, they can be stored outdoors in the garden. Dig the parsnips up with a fork, being careful not to damage them, and "heel" them in elsewhere. To heel, dig a shallow trench, bundle up the parsnips, and lay them close together, then cover up with soil. They take up far less space like this, can be dug up when they are needed, and will keep for a few more weeks.

Careful! Wear gloves when working with parsnips, because some people develop a rash when their skin comes in contact with the plants.

Grow Cabbages

Cabbages and their close relatives, such as sprouts, broccoli, and kale thrive in heavy, rich soils and sunny locations. Cabbages spend a relatively long time in the ground, but their vitamin-rich leaves are well worth the wait. As well as summer and autumn varieties, try growing winter and spring types for a year-round crop.

full sun

moist soil

Equipment

- Cabbage seeds
- Module trays
- Potting compost
- Dibber
- Watering can
- Bamboo canes
- String
- Trowel
- Fork
- Rake
- Insect-proof netting

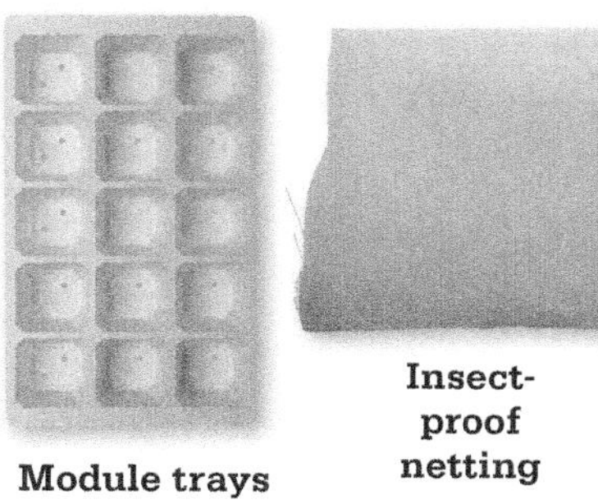

Summer and autumn cabbages *18–24 weeks until harvest*

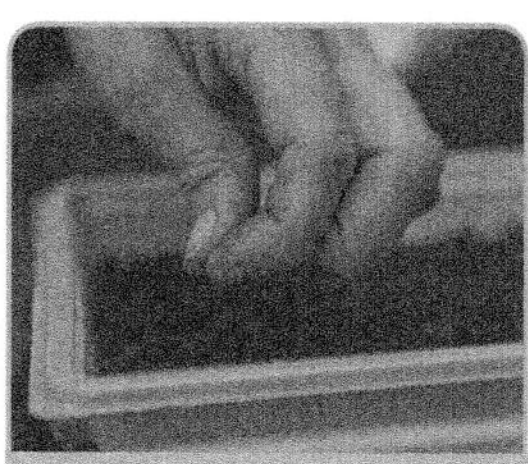

Sow seeds *under cover in early to mid-spring*

Plant out *in mid- to late spring once frosts have passed*

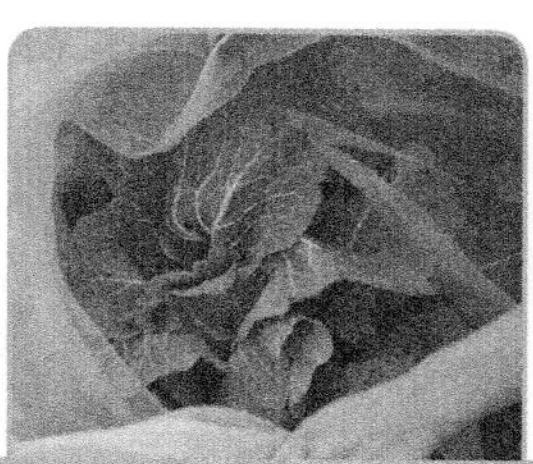

Protect plants *from pests using fine, insect-proof netting*

Harvest *crops throughout summer and into autumn*

1 Sow cabbage seeds into module trays or small plastic pots filled with general-purpose compost. Using a dibber, make a 1-cm (½-in) hole in each module or pot. Drop two or three seeds in each hole. Cover the seeds over with compost and water in well.

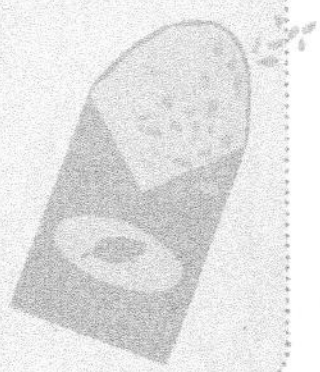

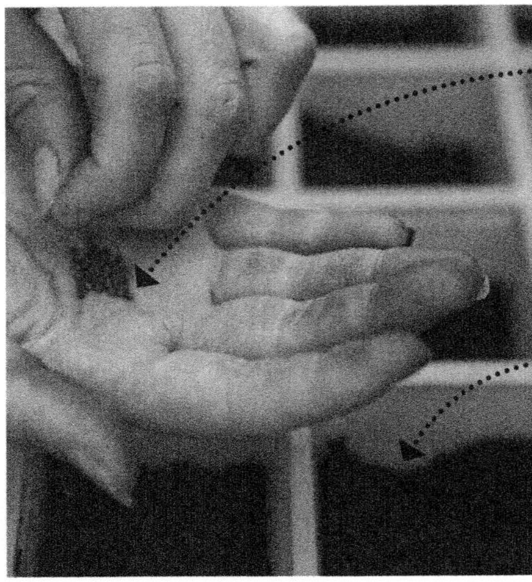

Tip the seeds into your hand to make it easy to control how many you sow

Cabbages are hungry plants, so use good-quality compost

When the seedlings look like this, they are ready to be planted out

2 The seeds should germinate within about 10 days, depending on the variety and time of year they are sown. Thin the cabbage seedlings out so that just the strongest and healthiest plant remains per pot or module.

Remember When the seedlings are about 8cm (3in) tall, they are ready to be planted outside.

3 Prior to planting out the seedlings, you'll need to thoroughly prepare the soil. Cabbages are hungry plants so will need plenty of manure dug into the ground. Water the seedlings, slide them from their pots, and plant 40cm (16in) apart.

Careful! Ensure that you don't damage the roots when planting out your seedlings.

Plant cabbages into rich, heavy soils containing well-rotted manure

Ensure the base of the stem is level with the soil

4 Water the young cabbages well as they start to grow. During hot spells in the summer they may need watering every day. Cabbage plants will also benefit from the occasional liquid feed in summer.

Careful! When watering in the summer, avoid splashing the leaves as this can scorch them.

Use a rose attached to the watering can to distribute the water gently around the plant

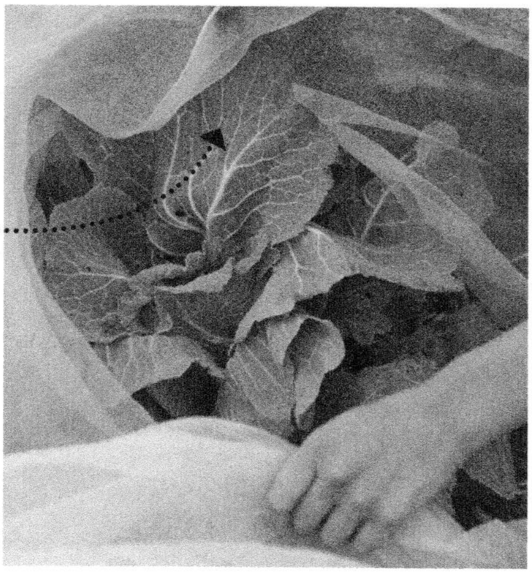

Use a very fine mesh to prevent pests getting to the plants

5 Place very fine mesh around the cabbages as they develop throughout the season. This should help keep away the three major pests: cabbage root fly, pigeons, and cabbage white caterpillars. Check the plants regularly for infestations.

Careful! If you find cabbage white caterpillars, remove the eggs and caterpillars by hand immediately.

6 Your cabbages will be ready to harvest about 30 weeks after sowing. They should be harvested by cutting through the base of their stem with a knife.

Tip Cabbages are large and bulky to store, so harvest the crop as and when needed – cabbages can stand in the ground for a few weeks until needed.

Harvest alternate cabbages along the row to allow the rest to continue maturing

Caring for your **Cabbages**

Cabbages come in a range of colours and shapes and are a very rewarding crop to grow, provided you can keep them safe from pests and disease.

The heart is the best part to eat – trim off the tough, outer leaves

To keep your cabbages looking this good you will need to protect them from pests

Once harvested cabbages can be left to re-sprout leaves from the stump

Things to watch out for...

Garden pests The worst culprits are pigeons, which can tear cabbages to shreds, so cover the plants up with a net to keep them safe. Cabbage white butterfly and cabbage root fly are the other pests to watch out for. Netting will deter butterflies, while a brassica collar (see p.128) will keep cabbage root fly from laying its eggs near your plants.

Clubroot If seedlings become stunted, wilted, or discoloured, it may be a sign of clubroot. This fungal disease causes swellings filled with spores on the roots of plants. The disease can survive in the soil for up to 20 years, so dig up and destroy infected plants and rotate crops in future years.

Dry soil Give these hungry plants a liquid feed every few weeks as they grow to keep them healthy. Water them daily during periods of drought.

Seasonal plantings It is possible to grow a year-round supply of cabbages, if you plan carefully. The name of the cabbage indicates when it will be ready to harvest. Spring cabbages are grown over winter and harvested early in the year. They are often grown closely together and harvested as young, tender crops. Summer and autumn cabbages are sown in spring and harvested in late summer, and cope well with hot conditions. Winter cabbages are often the ornamental type that can be used in potagers and bedding schemes, and are ready to harvest from late autumn onwards.

Also learn to grow ▸▸▸

How to grow **Calabrese**

full sun

moist soil

Equipment

- Calabrese seeds
- Well-rotted manure
- Bamboo canes and string
- Spade
- Rake
- Watering can

Confusingly, when gardeners speak of broccoli, they are usually referring to the purple-sprouting plant that produces edible florets. The green, large-headed vegetable referred to as broccoli in the supermarkets is known as calabrese.

PREPARING THE SOIL

Calabrese should be sown directly in the soil where it is to be grown. Prepare the soil before planting by digging it over thoroughly and removing any weeds. Add plenty of well-rotted manure or compost to the soil (see p.15).

SOWING

Sow the seeds in mid-spring. Stretch out a string between two canes and create a drill 1cm (½in) deep. Thinly sow the seeds into the drill. Carefully push back the soil on top of them and water them in well. Seedlings will appear about 10 days later. As the plants develop, they should be thinned out to a final spacing of 30cm (12in) between each plant.

CARE

As the plants grow, keep the soil free from weeds, which will compete with the seedlings for nutrients, water, and light. Keep the plants well watered to prevent fungal diseases.

TROUBLESHOOTING

The main pest to watch out for on calabrese, and other plants from the brassica family, is the cabbage root fly. It lays its eggs at the base of the plant and the emerging larvae munch on the root system. To protect your plants, place a collar at their base or lay carpet to prevent the eggs from being laid (see p.128). Cover the plants with a net to stop butterflies from laying their eggs nearby and to stop birds destroying the crop.

HARVESTING

Calabrese will be ready to harvest from midsummer to early autumn. Harvest when the flowerheads have developed but just before they actually open. Remove them using a sharp knife.

Grow Beans Up a Wigwam

Runner beans are tasty and incredibly productive crops that will continue to produce pods as you harvest them. Training the plants to scramble up a wigwam makes an attractive feature in the vegetable garden – these rustic constructions add height and structure, while the brightly coloured flowers give them an ornamental quality.

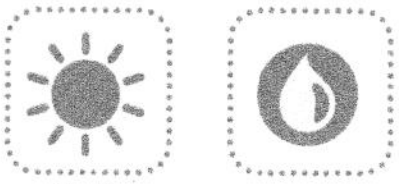

full sun

moist soil

Equipment

- Bean seeds
- General-purpose compost
- Plastic pots
- Large container
  such as a trug, with drainage holes
- 6 bamboo canes
- String
- Crocks
- Watering can

Bean seeds

General-purpose compost

Crocks

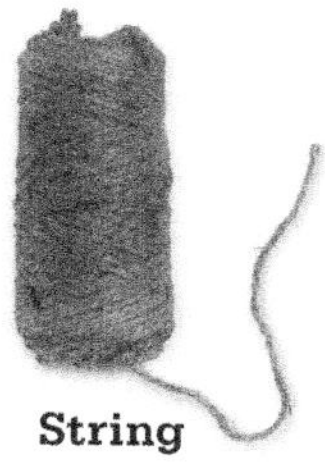

String

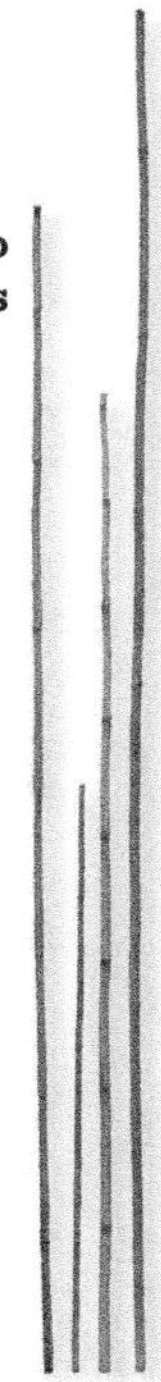

Bamboo canes

Watering can

Plastic pots

Large container

Runner beans *12–16 weeks until harvest*

Sow *seeds under cover in mid- to late spring*

Water *the seedlings well, especially in hot summer weather*

Harvest *the pods from midsummer and into autumn*

1 Sow runner bean seeds into small plastic pots in mid- to late spring; sow two seeds per pot. Use good quality general-purpose compost and keep the pots on a sunny windowsill or in a small greenhouse until the risk of frost has passed. Thin out the seedlings after a couple of weeks, leaving the healthiest, strongest plant per pot.

Seeds can either be sown directly into the soil or put into pots first

Create a sturdy structure by winding garden twine round the canes at 30-cm (12-in) intervals

Consider using hazel canes, which can look more attractive and rustic than these bamboo canes

2 Place crocks in the bottom of a large container with drainage holes and then fill with compost, mixing in some general-purpose fertilizer as you go. Insert 2-m (6½-ft) bamboo canes around the edge of your container, about 25cm (10in) apart. Using garden twine, tie together the canes at the top of the wigwam, and then secure at regular intervals down the length.

3 Arrange the plants around the edge of the container, making sure each plant has its own cane. Use a trowel to dig out a hole for each plant, then remove the plants from their pots and place into their holes. Firm them in and water well.

It is important the plants are well covered with compost to prevent them drying out

4 As the young plants start to grow, they can be trained up the bamboo canes; twist them around the canes and tie in place. Once they become established, they should begin to use their tendrils to climb on their own.

Careful! Monitor the plants for any signs of damage on the leaves, which could be caused by pests such as slugs or blackfly.

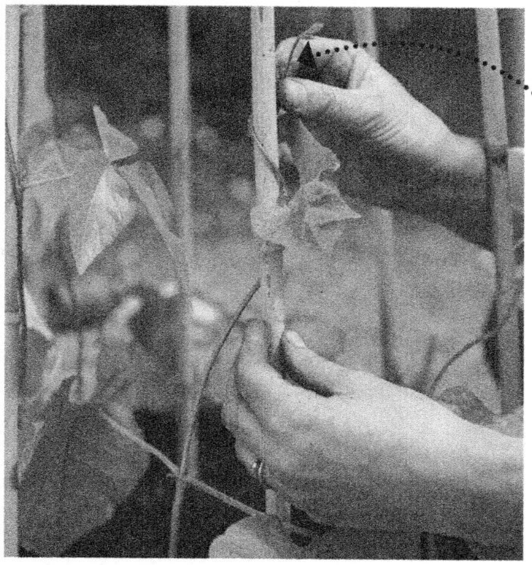

Use gardening twine to start training the shoots

The pretty flowers not only look good but will also attract bees to your garden

5 Keep checking the plants as they grow, as some wayward shoots will need retying and training in. Once the plants reach the top of the wigwam, remove the growing tips to stop them getting any taller.

Tip Remove any weeds, water the plants regularly, and give them a weekly liquid feed.

6 It takes about 12 weeks from sowing to harvesting. Pick regularly to keep the plants cropping – once they start they will provide a bumper crop over several months; each plant can produce about 1kg (2¼lb) of beans.

Careful! Do not leave the ripe beans on the plant too long, or they will become stringy.

Pick the beans regularly to encourage them to crop for longer

Caring for your **Runner Beans**

Fresh runner beans are a real treat in summer, and growing them is easy as long as you give them sturdy supports and pick them regularly to keep them cropping.

Things to watch out for...

Wayward plants Runner beans cling using their twining tendrils and need a good support system to keep them upright. Check that supports are sturdy and that plants are tied in as they grow to keep them neat and tidy. They can easily reach up to 3m (10ft) high, so pinch out the growing tips once they reach the top of their supports to keep them within bounds; smaller dwarf varieties are also available.

Dry soil When growing in a pot, runner beans will need watering most days, so keep an eye on the soil to make sure it doesn't dry out. Give the plants a weekly feed with liquid fertilizer.

Pests Keep an eye out for slugs and snails, which will munch on the young leaves at seedling stage – see p.67 for tips on how to deal with them. Mice can also dig up and eat seeds just after they have been sown, so protect them with a cloche.

Poor flowering Occasionally, beans can fail to set flowers, which means they won't produce a crop. Keeping the plant regularly watered and fed can help to prevent this. Generally, white and pink flowering types set flowers more readily than red.

Stringy pods Beans need to be picked every few days, otherwise the plant stops producing flowers. Pods that have been left for too long will be stringy and tough and should be thrown away.

Also learn to grow ▸▸▸

How to grow **Peas**

full sun

moist soil

Equipment

- Pea seeds
- Plastic guttering or plastic pots
- Dibber
- General-purpose compost
- Watering can
- Spade
- Rake
- Well-rotted manure
- Pea sticks or pea netting

Peas and beans belong to the same vegetable family, and like very similar growing conditions. Peas can be sown any time from early spring to late summer, and will provide you with a regular supply of pods if you sow them little and often.

SOWING

Get your seeds off to an early start in spring by taking a length of plastic guttering and filling it with general-purpose compost. Sow seeds 5cm (2in) apart and 5cm (2in) deep, then cover them up with compost. Alternatively, sow the seeds in individual pots. Water them well, and leave to germinate in a greenhouse or on a window ledge. Prepare the soil outside by digging it over, removing all weeds and incorporating some well-rotted manure. When the seedlings have appeared and the soil is warm enough, the plants can be slid out of the guttering into a shallow trench in the soil, or planted out, 5cm (2in) apart.

CARE

Peas are climbing plants and need supports to climb up. Push canes or twiggy pea sticks into the ground next to the seedlings. Alternatively, stretch pea netting or chicken wire upright next to them.

Keep the plants well watered as they grow, particularly when they begin to flower, as they may fail to produce flowers if the soil is dry.

Cover the plants with netting as birds love to strip the foliage and pods from the plants.

Pinch out the growing tips of the plants once they reach the top of their supports as some varieties can become very tall.

HARVESTING

Pea plants can keep producing pods if they are regularly picked, so keep checking the plants over. If you experience a glut, peas can be frozen, and sometimes taste even sweeter afterwards.

Grow Autumn Raspberries

Planting raspberries is a rewarding long-term project. They will be in the ground for about 15 years, so it is important to consider the location very carefully. Growing these sumptuous and mouth-watering fruits requires practical skill in erecting training systems as well as thinking one or two years ahead when it comes to pruning techniques.

full sun

light soil

Equipment

Raspberry canes
autumn-fruiting varieties

Well-rotted manure

Fork

Rake

Sturdy posts and string or wire

Trowel

Watering can

Secateurs

Gloves

Plant labels

General-purpose fertilizer

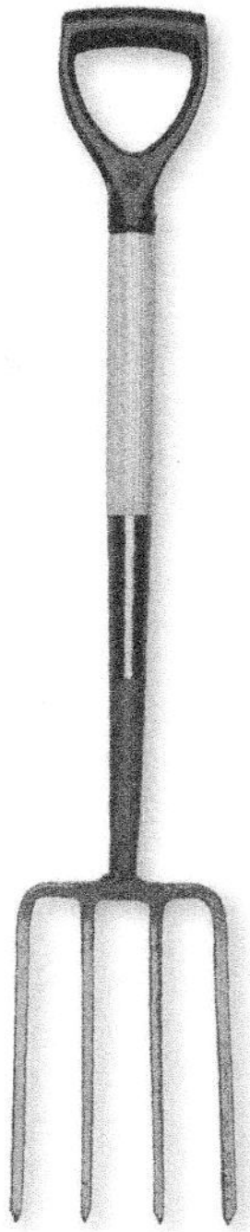

Fork

Rake

Posts

Well-rotted manure

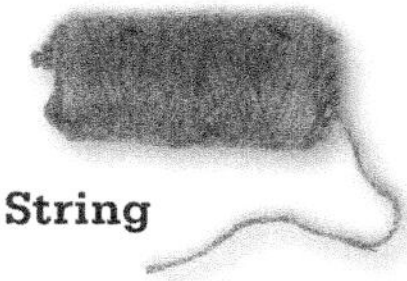

String

General-purpose fertilizer

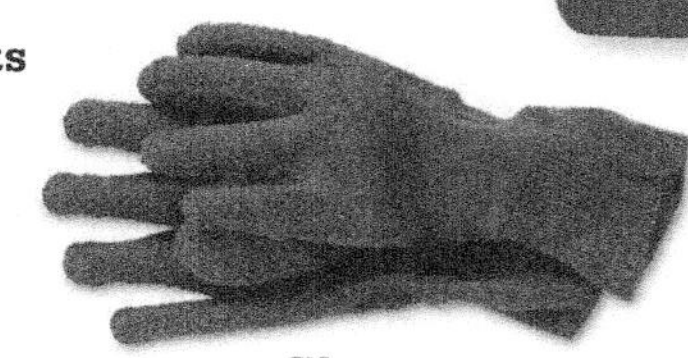

Gloves

Secateurs

Watering can

Trowel

Autumn raspberries *6–8 weeks until harvest*

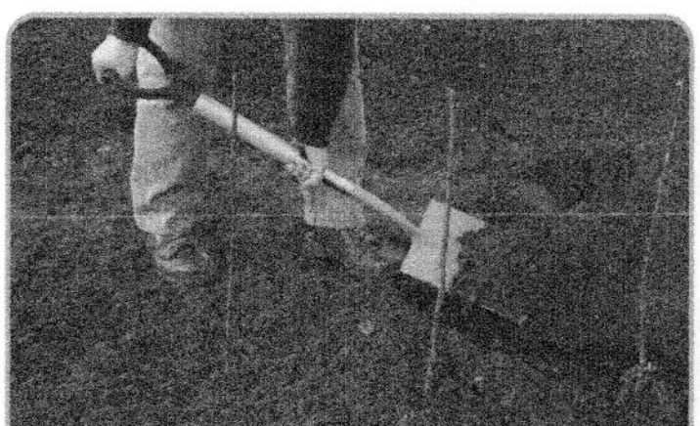

Plant *bare-root canes in winter; pot-grown canes all year*

Water *the canes well, especially in hot summer weather*

Harvest *fruit from late summer and into autumn*

1 Prepare your soil thoroughly and dig it over. Erect a support system by inserting sturdy posts at metre (3 foot) intervals along either side of where you plan to plant your row. Connect the posts with several secure lines of wire or string – you will tie your plants to these wires. Plant the raspberry canes about 40cm (16in) apart between the supports. The canes should be planted shallowly, roughly about 5cm (2in) deep.

Do not plant too deeply or the canes will rot

2 The leafy green shoots will start to appear in spring. Using secateurs, cut the original cane back to the lowest bud or shoot above ground level, being careful not to damage any of the new growth. As the canes grow, they will need to be securely attached to the wires with string.

Tip Feed the plants with some general fertilizer and keep them well weeded.

3 Recently planted canes will need watering about twice a week during the growing season. Raspberries are prone to produce suckers, which are new shoots that emerge from the base of the plant and grow away from the row of plants. Remove these as they will take nutrients and water away from the main plants.

Aim the water at the base of the plant, directly above its root system

4 Harvest the raspberries when they are plump and juicy. Autumn-fruiting raspberry plants should be left in the ground over winter and then pruned the following spring. Cut back all the fruited shoots to ground level.

Careful! If you are growing summer-fruiting types as well, keep them clearly separated, as these will need pruning in autumn rather than spring.

Caring for your **Raspberries**

Planting autumn-fruiting raspberries is easy. Looking after them for the next 15 years is slightly trickier. Make sure you support them well and prune them properly.

Things to watch out for...

Summer-fruiting varieties These raspberries fruit in summer and are pruned immediately after harvesting. They are more vigorous than autumn-fruiters and need a more extensive support system.

Yellow leaves Raspberries prefer slightly acid soil. If the leaves turn yellow this might be due to lime-induced chlorosis, which is caused by an alkaline soil – it can cause the plant to become deficient in vital nutrients, such as iron and manganese. Acidify the soil using sulphur chips.

Sagging stems Make sure you tie in your plants regularly and keep them well supported. Not only will this mean that plants have better airflow between the stems, reducing the chance of disease, but it is also easier to harvest fruit from a tidy plant.

Plant an Apple Tree in a Pot

Growing an apple tree in a pot is ideal if you want your own apples but are short on space. Choose a tree grown on a dwarf rootstock as these trees stay small and compact. A bud from the original variety is grafted onto roots from a less vigorous tree – it is the roots that mainly govern how large the tree will become.

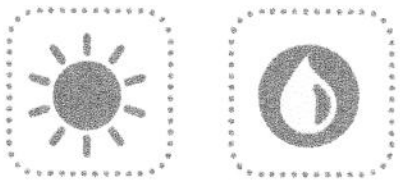

full sun **light soil**

Equipment

- Apple tree on dwarf rootstock such as M26 or MM106
- Large, frost-proof container
- Crocks
- General-purpose compost
- Controlled-release fertilizer
- Cane and string
- Watering can
- Liquid feed
- Secateurs

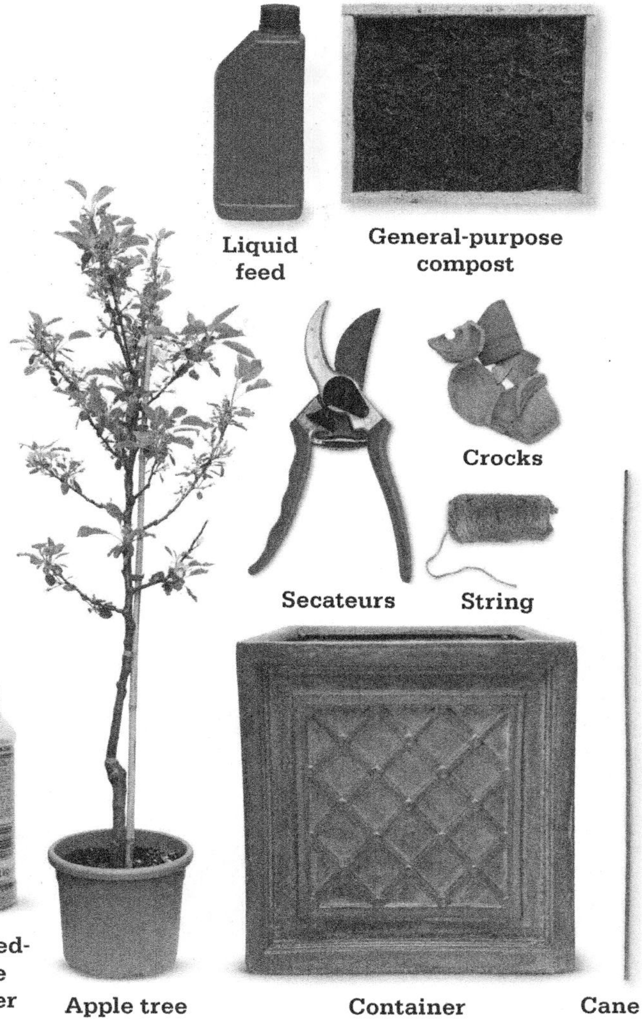

Apples *14–20 weeks until harvest*

Plant *bare-root trees in winter; pot-grown trees all year*

Water *the tree well after planting and over the summer*

Thin *the fruitlets in midsummer to produce larger crops*

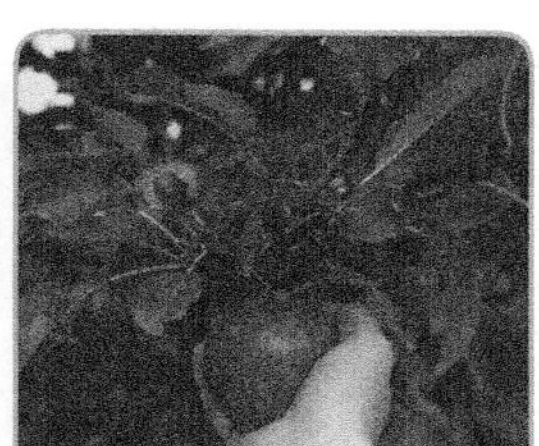

Harvest *the fruits from late summer into autumn*

1 Soak the apple tree thoroughly in a bucket of water for a few hours prior to planting. The tree should ideally be grown on a semi-dwarfing rootstock such as M26 or MM106, so that the tree remains a compact size.

Tip It is important that the root ball is allowed to take up as much water as possible, as it will be harder to thoroughly soak it once it is planted in its container.

Apple trees produce attractive blossom as well as delicious fruit

Soak the roots of the tree prior to planting

Choose a frost-resistant container

Covering the drainage holes with crocks prevents the roots from rotting

2 Ensure the container for the apple tree is frost-proof. It should be about 40cm (16in) wide and have drainage holes in the bottom. Prepare the container by placing crocks in the bottom to aid drainage.

Tip Make sure you have put the container into its final position before weighing it down with compost and the plant.

3 Add a good-quality general-purpose compost into the container. Mix in controlled-release fertilizer as you go – it will supply the plant with essential nutrients when it needs them.

Careful! When filling the container, make sure that you leave enough space for the volume of the root ball.

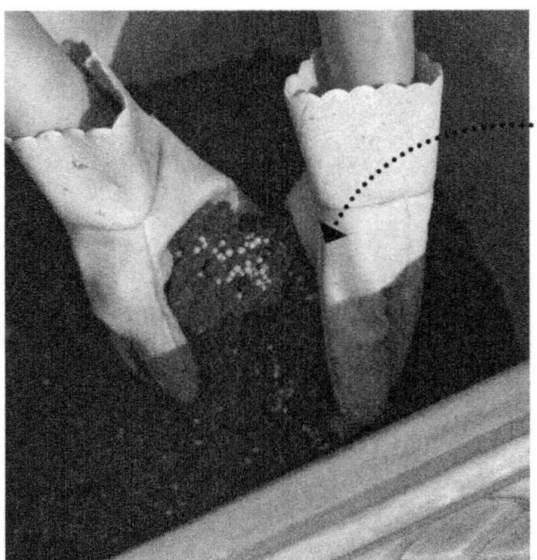

Wear gloves when handling the fertilizer granules

4 Gently remove the tree from the pot and place it in the compost, making sure the top of the root ball is just below the rim of the container.

Tip Tease out the roots before planting to make sure they spread out and grow strongly into the compost, rather than growing inwards and "strangling" the tree.

These fibrous roots should be teased out before planting

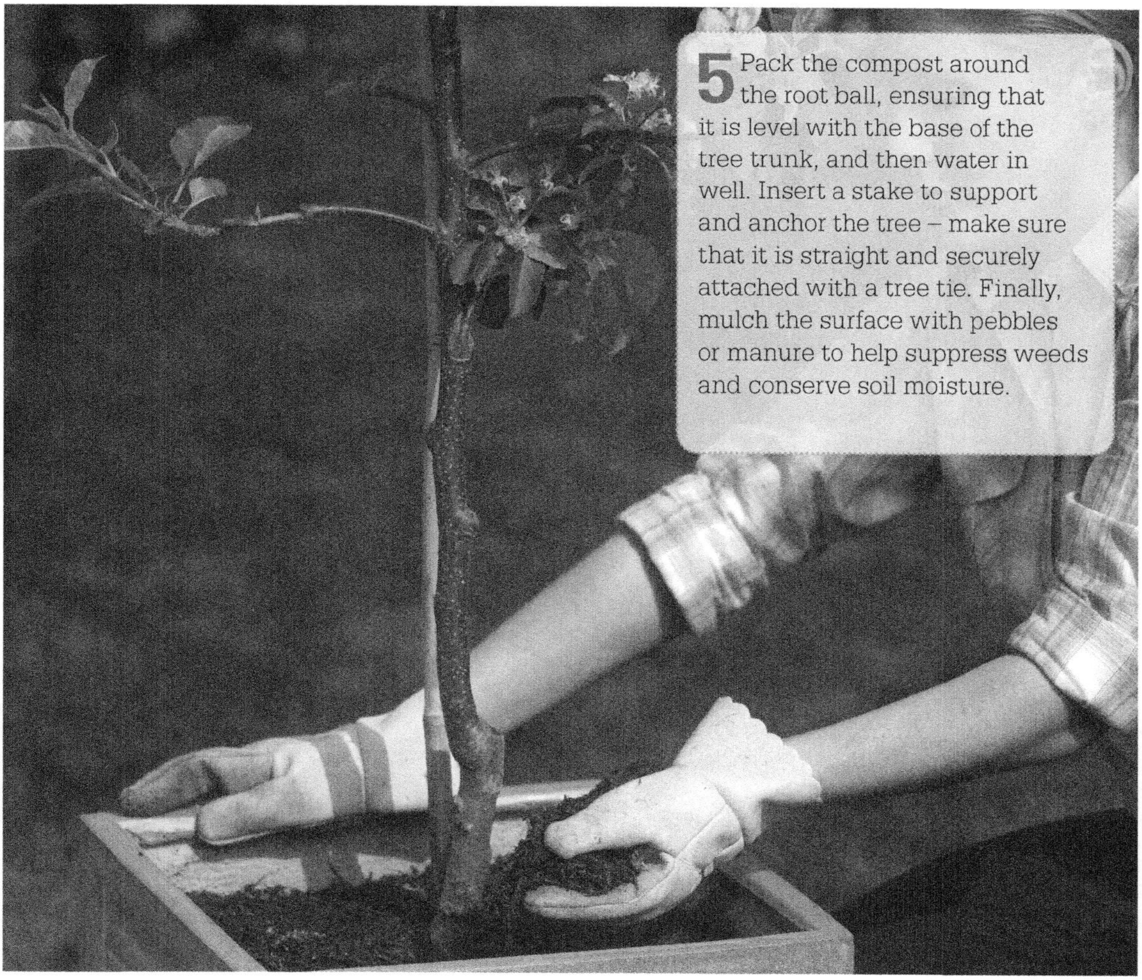

5 Pack the compost around the root ball, ensuring that it is level with the base of the tree trunk, and then water in well. Insert a stake to support and anchor the tree – make sure that it is straight and securely attached with a tree tie. Finally, mulch the surface with pebbles or manure to help suppress weeds and conserve soil moisture.

Caring for your **Apple Tree**

Apple trees in containers make fantastic features for patios and balconies. Techniques such as pruning and thinning the fruit will help the tree to thrive.

Things to watch out for...

Dry soil Apple trees grown in containers should be placed in a sheltered position in full sun, which will mean they are prone to drying out. Keep them well watered and feed them once a week during the growing season with a liquid feed such as tomato fertilizer.

Birds Place a net over the apple tree in summer to prevent birds pecking at the fruit.

Congested branches Apples trees should have a light prune each winter to remove any crossing or damaged branches.

An excess of fruit For the best crops of fruit, apples should be thinned in midsummer – reduce clusters of fruit down to just one or two apples.

Thickening trunks Check the tree ties once a year and loosen them slightly if it looks like they might damage the growing trunk.

Also learn to grow ▸▸▸

How to plant a **Fig Tree in a Pot**

Equipment

- Fig tree
- Good-quality soil-based compost
- Frost-resistant container
- Crocks
- Stake and tree tie
- Watering can
- Liquid feed

SUITABILITY

Fig trees are easier to grow than you might think. Despite their associations with the Mediterranean, the trees are very hardy and can tolerate low temperatures. The difficulty is getting them to fruit, as this requires sunshine and warmth. Figs are well suited to growing in a pot. In fact, they will produce more fruit if their roots are restricted than if planted in the open ground. The restriction forces the plant to reproduce by producing fruit rather than developing lots of leafy growth.

PLANTING

Figs should be planted in frost-resistant containers with a diameter of about 40cm (16in). Ensure the container has drainage holes and place crocks over them. Plant trees into free-draining, soil-based compost and water them in well.

CARE

Fig trees will need watering daily during the summer months as the container will drain quickly. They will fruit better if given a weekly liquid feed and benefit from a compost mulch each spring. Figs should be re-potted into fresh compost every few years, but resist the urge to give them a larger pot, as they fruit best with restricted roots.

FRUITING

Fruit is produced at the tips of the shoots. In cooler climates, figs only produce one crop of fruit a year, which is formed from fruitlets that overwinter and crop the following summer. Remove any newly formed fruit at the end of summer as it will not survive over the winter. Protect the fruit from birds and wasps using netting.

PRUNING

Minimal pruning is required on a fig tree. Occasionally older wood should be removed in winter, with younger wood left as a replacement. Pinch out growing tips in spring to encourage the formation of more fruitlets, and trim back any leaves that shade the swelling fruit in summer.

Plant Blackcurrants

The jet-black berries dangling from the branches of a blackcurrant bush make a great addition to any kitchen garden. Blackcurrants are grown as stool bushes, which means they are planted deep into the soil and their shoots emerge straight from the ground.

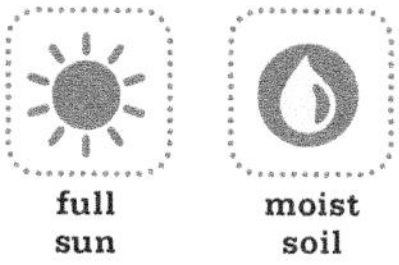

Equipment

- Blackcurrant plant
- Fork
- Rake
- Spade
- Well-rotted manure
- Canes and string
- Controlled-release fertilizer
- Watering can
- Plant labels

Blackcurrants *10–12 weeks until harvest*

Plant *bare-root plants in winter; pot-grown plants all year round*

Support *the plants with canes as the fruit develops*

Harvest *strigs of berries from mid- to late autumn*

1 Dig a hole double the width of the blackcurrant plant's root ball and about 10cm (4in) deeper than the depth of the pot. Use a planting stick placed across the hole to check the depth against the plant's stem – the plant needs to be slightly deeper in the ground than in its pot. Mix compost or well-rotted manure with the soil from the hole. Use this mix to backfill around the root ball.

Firm in close to the stem, but be careful not to damage it

2 Firm the plant in using your hands or feet, and then rake the ground level afterwards. Give the plant a thorough soaking using a watering can with a fine rose attachment. Sprinkle a general-purpose fertilizer around the root area and mulch with well-rotted manure.

Tip If you are planting more than one, space them 1.5m (5ft) apart.

3 As the plant grows, it will need to be kept well watered, especially during its first summer, and it will also need regular feeding. Pull out weeds by hand rather than using a hoe, as this could damage the roots. Apply a mulch of manure in spring.

Careful! The flowers may need protection with garden fleece in spring, if frost is forecast.

A liquid feed will keep the leaves looking green and healthy

A generous dollop of manure around the plant will prevent weeds from germinating

Support the branches with canes and string to prevent branches snapping

Keep the base of the plant free from weeds and well watered during summer

4 When the plants start to produce fruit the branches will need support to prevent them from snapping under the weight. The easiest method is to make a frame: insert four bamboo canes around the plant and tie them together with string.

Careful! Place a net over the plants as the fruit ripens to stop birds devouring the crop.

Caring for your **Blackcurrants**

Blackcurrants look just as dramatic and impressive as any display of flowers and are also attractive to birds, so make sure you protect them with netting.

Blackcurrants are easy to grow but the tiny berries can be tricky to pick

Blackcurrants make a healthy snack and are packed full of vitamin C

Things to watch out for...

Ripe berries These are irresistible to birds, so use netting to protect them. Picking the tiny berries can be difficult because they are so small, so use scissors to cut whole strigs (lengths of stems), once the fruits have turned black.

Weak growth Blackcurrants need a heavy, fertile soil with a high nitrogen content to encourage lots of new shoots to emerge each year from the base of the bush. Each spring, apply a fertilizer such as sulphate of ammonia before mulching heavily around the root system. Water the plants well.

Spindly, congested stems Blackcurrants should be pruned each year during winter by removing about a third of the old, spindly wood from the base of the plant.

Also learn to grow ▸▸▸

Plant **White- and Redcurrants**

full sun or part shade

light soil

Equipment

- A white- or redcurrant bush
- Well-rotted manure or compost
- Spade
- Bamboo canes and string
- Secateurs
- Netting

White- and redcurrants are the same plant, simply producing different coloured fruit. They can be grown equally well in shade or sun, which makes them ideal for growing in north-facing gardens and patios, where other crops may struggle.

PLANTING

Currants should be planted in autumn when the ground is still warm. They need fertile soil that has been enriched with well-rotted manure or compost. Plant them so that they sit at the same height in the ground as they did in their pot. Use netting to protect the juicy fruits from birds.

PRUNING

Plants should be grown as an open-centred bush on a small stem about 20cm (8in) off the ground. The centre of the canopy should be free from branches and four or five branches should form the main structure of the bush, making a goblet shape. Currants can also be grown as vertical cordons (see pp.180–181).

Prune the currants in winter, ensuring that no new shoots are growing across the centre of the plant and that diseased wood is removed. In summer, prune back the new growth to five leaves to allow better air circulation and so that sunlight can reach the fruit (see pp.176–179).

Whitecurrants

Redcurrants

Plant **Gooseberries**

full sun or part shade

light soil

Equipment

- A gooseberry bush
- Well-rotted manure or compost
- Spade
- Bamboo canes and string
- Secateurs
- Netting
- Posts and wires

Gooseberries grow in exactly the same way as white- and redcurrants, and so their treatment is the same too. They should also be pruned in the same way as currants, as they fruit on old wood and the base of new wood. They tolerate shade, so can be planted in north-facing gardens.

PLANTING

The plants can be grown as free-standing bushes and should be spaced 1m (3ft) apart. Alternatively they can be trained. Before planting, erect a training system of three horizontal wires, placed parallel and strained between stout posts. Dig a hole that matches the depth that the plant was at in its container. Place the plant in the hole, firm it down, and water in well. For cordons (see p.180), plant 35cm (14in) apart and attach to vertical bamboo canes tied to the wires.

PRUNING CORDONS

Prune bushes as for currants (see facing page). Remove any crossing, diseased, or damaged wood. Prune cordons twice a year. In summer, the new growth should be cut back to five leaves from the stem. In winter, cut back the new growth to two buds. Do not prune the topmost shoot, instead train it up the cane until it has reached the top wire.

CARE

Keep gooseberries well watered in their first year, and feed and mulch them every following year in spring. As the fruit starts to ripen, net the plants to prevent bird damage.

TROUBLESHOOTING

Look out for the hairy caterpillars of gooseberry sawfly, which can strip the leaves from a plant within days. Remove the caterpillars by hand as soon as you spot them. Gooseberries are susceptible to American mildew, so choose resistant varieties such as 'Invicta' and keep the plant regularly watered (see p.66).

How to **Protect Plants from Pests**

There are simple ways to guard your plants from pests and many do not require expensive or specialist equipment – you can make them at home from recycled materials. The most important defence is to know your enemies so that you understand the best ways to deter them.

Netting

Common garden pests, such as birds, mice, and squirrels often strike when the crops are ready for harvesting and at their tastiest, but they can be deterred using netting. Hang the netting from canes to keep it off the crops and make sure there are no holes or gaps as the pests will quickly find them. Peg the nets to the ground to make them completely secure. Some crops, such as cabbages, should be covered with very fine netting or fleece, which will keep out cabbage white butterflies.

Brassica Collars

Cabbage root fly is a common pest for brassicas such as cabbages and will attack the roots of the plants and cause them to die. There is no effective insecticide so the best defence is a "brassica collar", as placing a barrier around the base of the stems stops the cabbage root fly from landing and laying its eggs. Purpose-made collars can be bought from reputable garden centres or you can make your own. Cardboard discs or squares of carpet can be used and are just as effective.

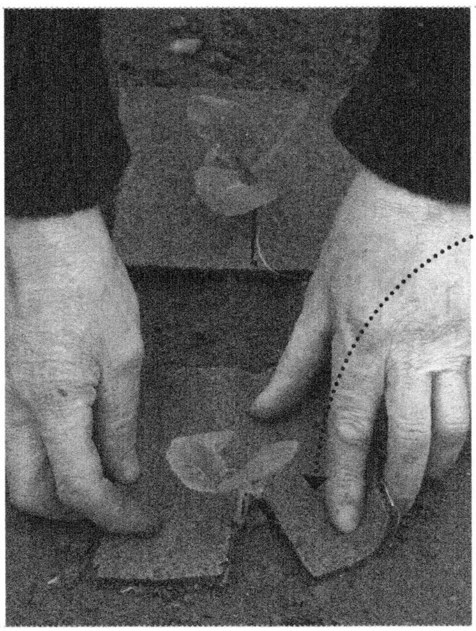

Cut a slit in the square so that it can be positioned without damaging the seedling

Recycle old foil or shiny wrapping paper as a free bird deterrent

Shiny objects

A simple method of deterring birds from attacking fruit and vegetables is to hang shiny objects nearby that will sway in the wind and shimmer in the sunlight – the flashing light will scare off the birds. Hang old CDs, strips of foil, or shiny paper from pieces of string suspended around your garden.

Purpose-built structures

It is possible to buy purpose-built structures that can be placed over individual plants. The beauty of these structures is that they are quick to use and can be stacked easily for storage in the shed. In winter and spring they can be used as cloches for frost protection by wrapping polythene around them. You can even make these yourself from chicken wire.

These structures will protect crops from bird damage

Fleece

Birds are not the only pests to fly around the vegetable patch. Carrot fly is a major problem too. Its larvae tunnel their way through the crops, making them inedible. One method of deterring them is to erect very fine fleece around your crops. Make sure that the barrier is at least 60cm (24in) high and secure at the bottom, as the carrot fly can't fly high enough to get over this barrier.

3

Take It Further

This final chapter will introduce you to a new range of delicious – often gourmet – crops, including tender asparagus, glistening aubergines, juicy plums, and jewel-like blueberries. Some of these crops require special care and attention, while others are perennial, and will repay the long term investment of your time and space. But they are all worth the extra effort, and are a great addition to any kitchen garden.

In this section learn to grow:

Leeks
see pp.138–143

Aubergines
see pp.144–149

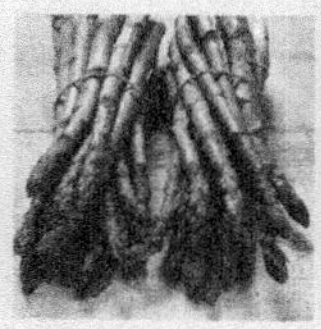

Asparagus
see pp.150–153

Artichokes
see pp.154–157

Herbs
see pp.158–163

Blueberries
see pp.164–167

Plums
see pp.170–174

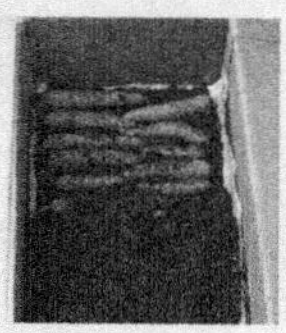

Storage
see pp.182–185

Planning a Kitchen Garden

Careful planning is essential to kitchen gardening. In restricted spaces, keep it simple and manageable – choose small amounts of a wider range of crops and only choose crops that you really enjoy eating. The plot plans given here are based on a 3x3m (10x10ft) square plot, but if your space is not this size or shape, take inspiration from these plans and adjust them for your own garden.

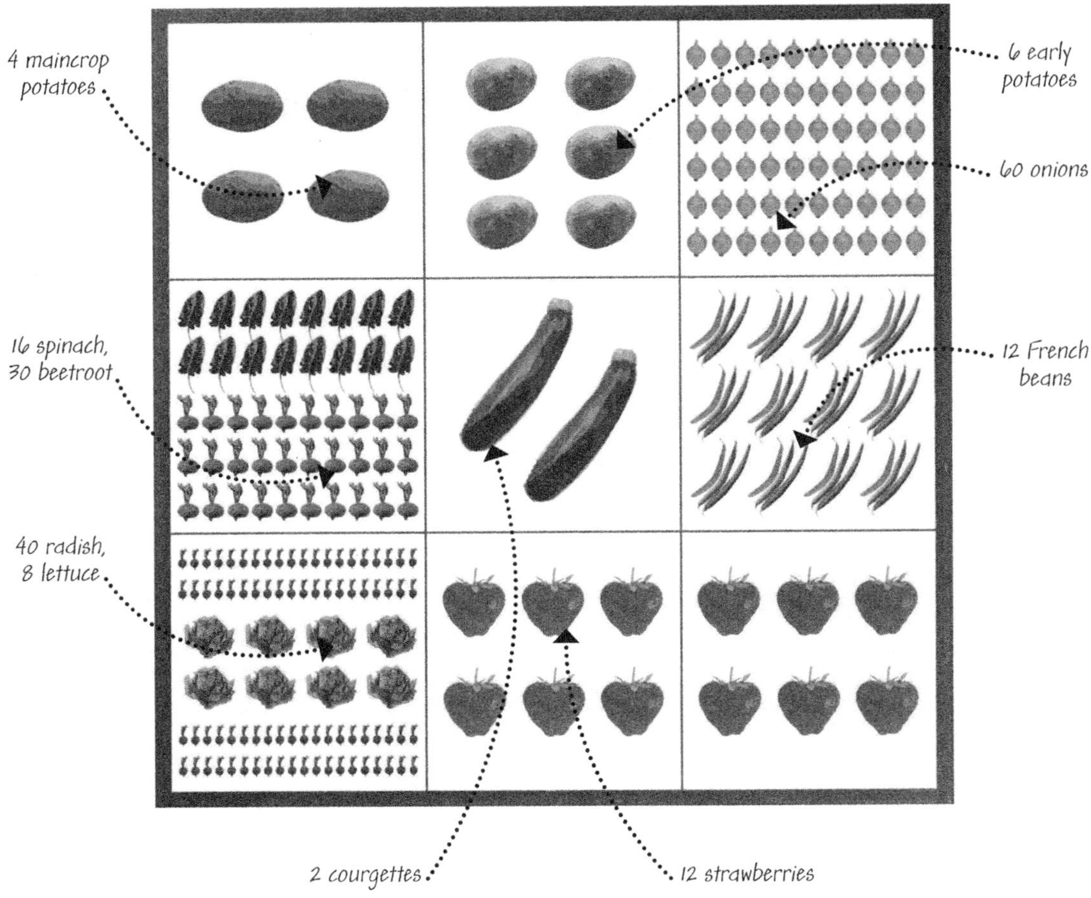

The easy-to-grow plot

This simple planting plan provides the staple crops of potatoes, onions, and beans along with delicious, quick-growing salad crops such as radishes, beetroot, and lettuce. Reliable courgette and spinach plants will produce exciting options for stir-fries, and strawberries will provide a delicious treat in early to midsummer. All these crops are easy to grow and make an excellent starting point if you are planning a vegetable plot for the first time. Position the crops that you will harvest first – here the speedy salad crops – on the outside edge of your space, so that they are easy to reach without disturbing your other crops.

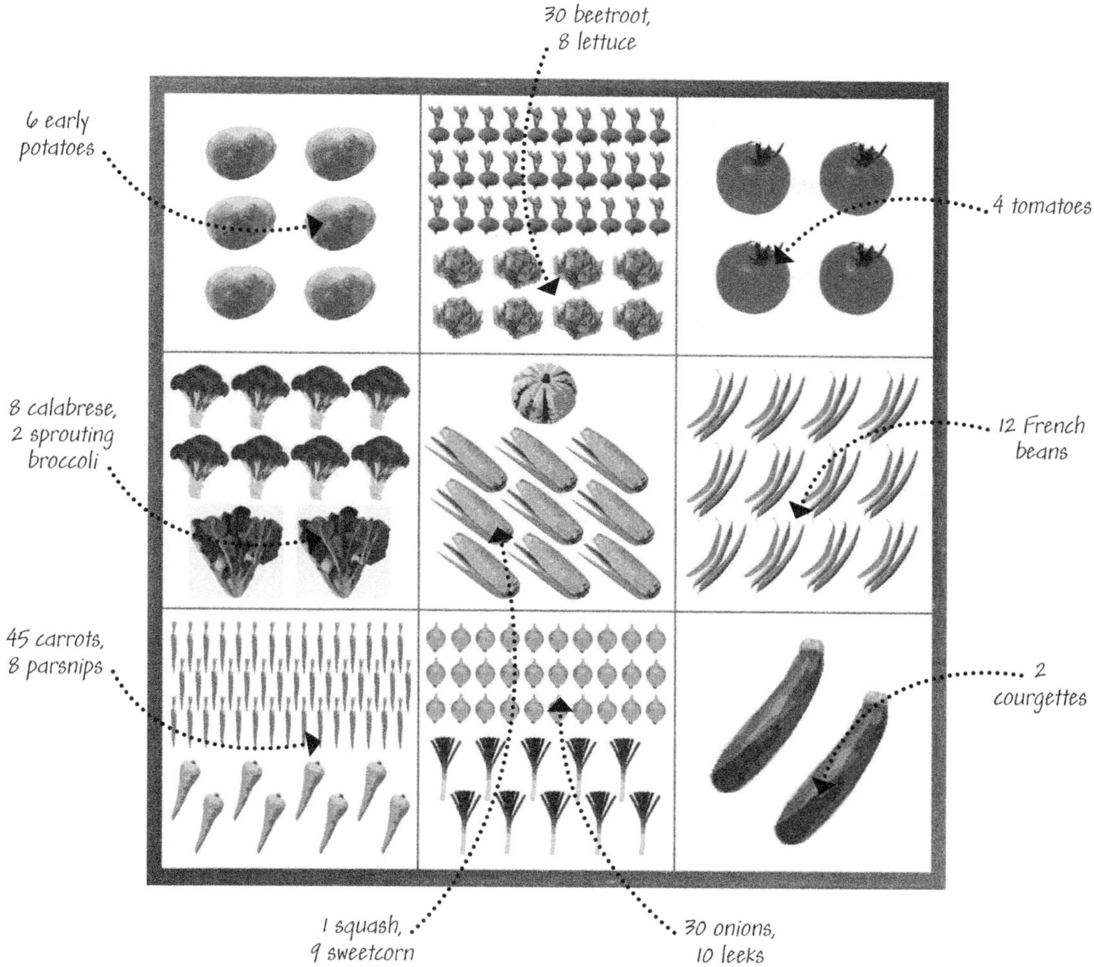

The family plot

If you want to be adventurous and are trying to expand the list of vegetables your family eats, try this planting combination. This plot is designed for maximum productivity in a small space: a squash is planted on the ground underneath the tall sweetcorn plants, as it thrives in this environment, allowing you to maximize your growing space. Some of the crops in this plan are simple to grow, such as the lettuces and tomatoes, while others, such as the sweetcorn are more difficult, making this an ideal plot for the family to grow together. Onions, tomatoes, and carrots are probably the most popular ingredients for family meals, and this plan will provide you with plenty, while the two courgette plants will supply an abundance of vegetables for more exciting recipes. Winter crops such as the calabrese, leeks, parsnips, and purple-sprouting broccoli will provide food later in the season, after most other crops have been harvested. If you want to grow some sweet treats for summer desserts, add strawberries or redcurrants to the combination.

Crop Rotation

To avoid a build-up of crop-specific pests and diseases in the soil and to prevent a depletion of certain nutrients, it is important to grow groups of annual crops in different parts of the vegetable patch year on year. Certain types of crop have similar needs and can be grouped together into three distinct "years", although some people choose to create five rotations.

Beetroots

Carrots

Potatoes

Radishes

Year 1: root vegetables

The root vegetable group includes potatoes, beetroots, carrots, leeks, lettuces, radishes, onions, parsnips, and spinach. Grow these in the ground after harvesting and clearing the brassica family of vegetables. These crops do not have a very high requirement for nitrogen, so are ideal to follow the brassicas, which will have depleted some of the nitrogen from the soil. The following year, replace the root family with peas, beans, and fruiting vegetables.

Beans

Tomatoes

Year 2: peas and beans

Peas, beans, and fruiting vegetables are usually planted in the space where the root family grew the year before. This group also includes aubergines, celery, courgettes, pumpkins, sweetcorn, chilli, and tomatoes.

Peas and beans absorb nitrogen from the air and "fix" it in the soil, creating a rich environment that benefits the crops that will occupy the space the following year: nitrogen-hungry brassicas will replace them.

Cauliflower

Cabbage

Year 3: cabbage family

Often referred to as brassicas, this group includes calabrese, purple-sprouting broccoli, cauliflower, Brussels sprouts, kale, swedes, and turnips. These crops need a nitrogen-rich site so should be planted into soil vacated by the peas and beans family. It is particularly important to move this group of crops around, as they are very susceptible to soil-borne diseases such as clubroot, for which there is no cure and can remain in the soil for years.

How to make **Compost and Leaf Mould**

A compost bin is useful if you plan on growing more than just a few vegetables in pots. Compost bins don't need much space and can easily be tucked into a corner of your plot. Alternatively, consider making leaf mould, which can be added to the soil to improve its structure.

Recycling kitchen waste

Filling up the compost bin

Turning the compost

Composting

A compost heap should be a mix of carbon-based material, such as shredded newspaper and wood chips, and nitrogen-based matter, such as kitchen waste, which prevents the compost turning smelly and slimy. Keep the compost heap warm by leaving a lid on it – you can make one from cardboard if you need to – and turn it over every few weeks. Within two to three months the mixture will have broken down into rich, sweet-smelling compost.

Tip Fallen leaves are abundant in autumn, and are absolutely free! They can be transformed into lovely, soil-improving leaf mould.

Making leaf mould

Leaf mould usually has fewer nutrients than compost, but is fantastic for improving soil structure. Rake up leaves in autumn and place them in a bin liner. Alternatively, use a rotary mower to gather them up off the lawn, as shredded leaves will break down faster. If the leaves are dry, add water to speed up decomposition. Store them in a cool, dry place and shake up the bag occasionally. The process takes about two years.

Grow Leeks

With their delicious mild onion flavour, leeks are one of the stalwarts of the winter vegetable garden. They provide a good alternative to brassicas when there is little else available to harvest, and they can be pulled young, to produce tender "baby" leeks.

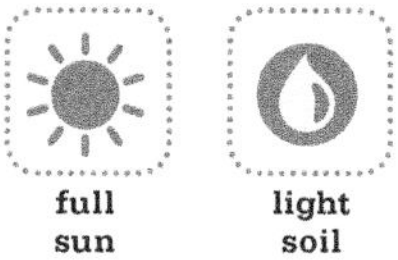

Equipment

- Leek seeds
- Potting compost
- Trowel
- Biodegradable modules
- Watering can
- Hand fork
- Scissors
- Fork and rake
- Well-rotted manure
- Dibber
- Liquid feed

Leeks *30–32 weeks until harvest*

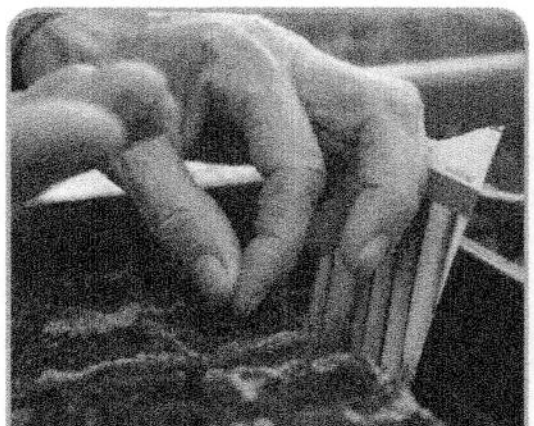

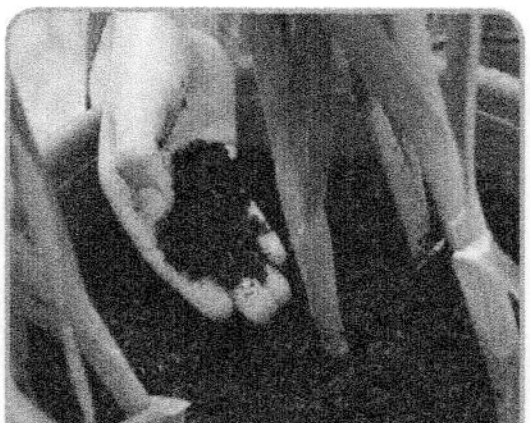

- **Sow seed** *in early to mid-spring and keep warm under cover*
- **Plant out** *seedlings in late spring to early summer*
- **Earth up** *the stems as they grow to block out the light*
- **Harvest** *from late summer through to wintertime*

1 Leeks can be sown under cover in midwinter into biodegradable modules or pots filled with seed compost. They must be watered in well and will need to be kept at a temperature of about 10°C (50°F), otherwise they will not germinate.

Tip Biodegradable pots allow you to plant out the seedlings without disturbing their root systems.

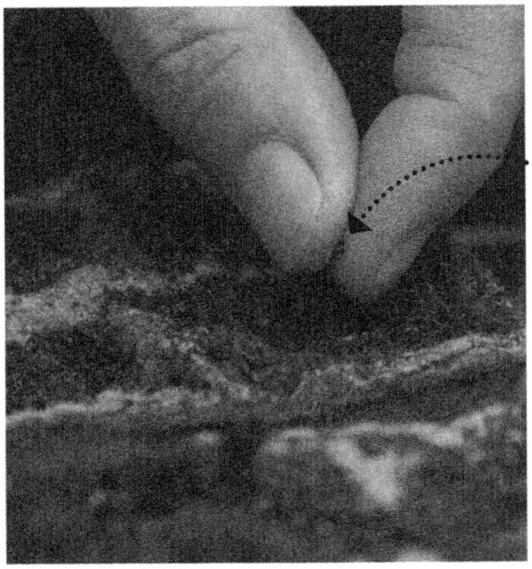

Sow three or four seeds into each module.

Check the leeks have an established root system before planting

2 Once the seedlings are large enough and the weather has warmed up in late spring, plant them outside into a sheltered seed bed – a temporary outdoor growing location – to allow them to develop into bigger plants.

Tip Water the seedlings in well to encourage them to develop fully.

3 When the seedlings have grown about 25cm (10in) tall they can be planted out into their final growing position. Use a hand fork to gently lift them out of the soil, being careful not to break their delicate leaves or roots.

Remember Dig over the vegetable bed and add plenty of well-rotted manure before you transfer your leek plants.

Lift seedlings ready to be planted in their final position

4 Before planting out the leeks, trim their roots to 2.5cm (1in). This makes it easier to slot them into their holes and will also stimulate them to grow quickly once they are in the soil.

5 Use a large dibber to create planting holes about 2.5cm (1in) wide, 15cm (6in) deep, and 25cm (10in) apart. Drop the leeks into them so that just their tips stick out of the top.

Tip If you want to grow "baby" leeks, which are harvested when they are still small and tender, space seedlings 10cm (4in) apart.

6 Do not push the soil back around the seedlings but instead water them in thoroughly, allowing the soil to loosely crumble around the stems of the leeks. The plants must be kept well watered while the stems are swelling.

Why? Leaving space around the seedlings allows their stems to swell easily as they grow.

There should be space around the seedlings

Allow the water to pool a little around the seedling

7 As the leeks grow, regularly push the soil up around the base of the stems with a trowel. This process, known as blanching, blocks out the light and helps to keep the plants white and tender, as well as making them more stable. Once the leeks are fully grown, harvest them using a fork.

Caring for your **Leeks**

Leeks are related to the onion family, but rather than producing bulbs they form tender white stems. Earth up the plants and water regularly to encourage a healthy crop.

Things to watch out for...

Leek moth and onion fly The caterpillars of leek moth pest bore into the leaves and stems of plants, while onion fly attacks the roots, causing plants to rot. Remove and destroy any infected plants. Don't be disheartened though, covering the plants with insect-proof mesh will help to deter these pests. Leek rust is another common problem, but resistant varieties are available.

Weeds Regularly hoe around the plants to prevent the growth of weeds, which compete for nutrients and can affect the size of your crop.

Extra space Leeks can remain in the ground for most of the winter, until you are ready to harvest them, but if you need to use their growing space for other crops they can be lifted and "heeled in" elsewhere: dig them up and place them in a new hole with fresh soil around their roots.

Grow Aubergines

Aubergine plants traditionally needed a warm, sunny, sheltered site or a greenhouse in order to produce fully ripe fruits. However, with the introduction of modern hybrids and grafted varieties these fascinating plants can now be grown outdoors even in cooler climates.

full sun **moist soil**

Equipment

- Aubergine seeds
- Plastic pots, small and large
- Potting compost
- Watering can
- Fork
- General-purpose compost
- Bamboo canes and string
- Liquid feed
- Plant labels
- Trowel

Aubergines *24–28 weeks until harvest*

Sow seeds *under cover in early spring and keep them warm*

Plant out *in late spring once frosts have passed*

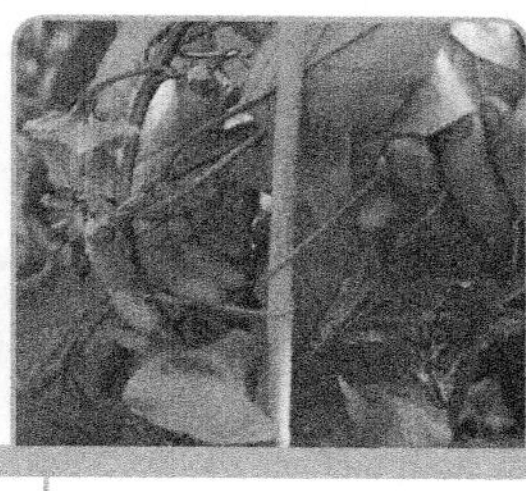

Support *the plants as the fruit develops and becomes heavy*

Harvest *the aubergines from late summer into autumn*

1 Fill small plastic pots or plastic tray modules with seed compost in early spring. Firm the soil down and lightly water prior to sowing the seeds.

Tip Although aubergines can be bought as young plants in spring, it is cheaper to grow them from seed and start them off indoors.

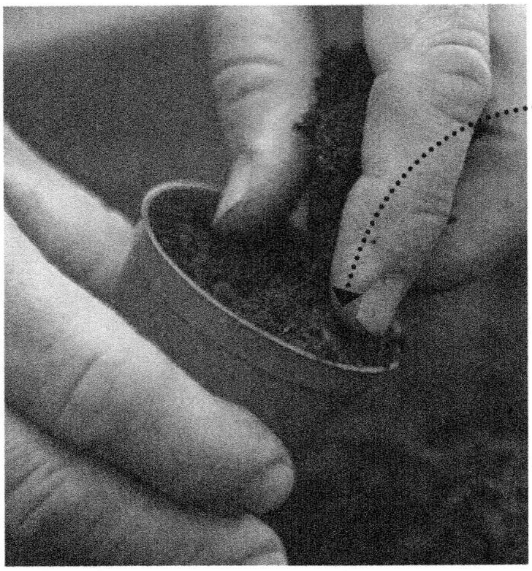

2 Sow one seed per pot or module. Place the seed on the surface, then gently push it under the surface to a depth of 1cm ($^{1}/_{2}$in) using a dibber, pencil, or your finger. Top up with compost. Water well and place the pots in a heated propagator, in a greenhouse, or on a sunny windowsill.

3 Seeds should start to germinate in about seven to 10 days. Once the seedlings are about 6cm (2½in) tall, remove them from the propagator and leave them in the greenhouse or on a windowsill until they are ready to be potted on.

Remember Keep checking on the plant to make sure that it hasn't grown too big for its pot, and regularly water it.

Take the seedlings out of the propagator when they are this height

Keep checking the moisture of the soil and water if the surface feels dry

Push the smaller pot into the larger one to create a planting hole for the seedling

4 When roots appear through the drainage holes in the bottom of the pot, it is time to plant up into a bigger container. Plant into 30-cm (12-in) wide pots filled with multi-purpose compost.

Tip If you are growing the plants on in a greenhouse, this larger pot will be their final location.

5 Once the risk of all late frosts has passed, the plants can be planted out. Harden them off and plant them in a warm, sheltered position in well-prepared soil. Give them a spacing of between 60–75cm (24–30in).

Remember Prior to planting out, harden the aubergines off in a porch or cold frame (see p.74).

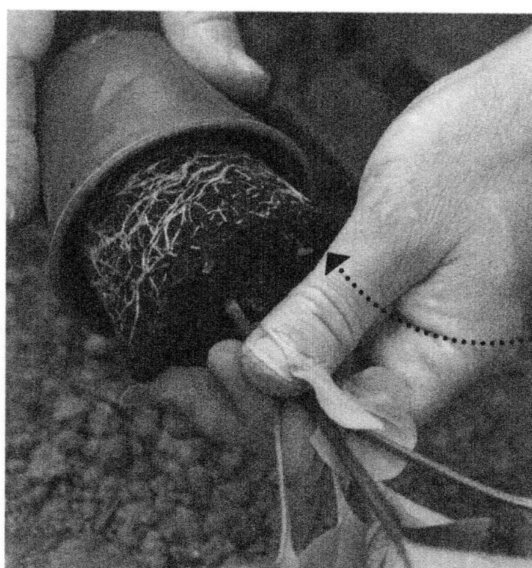

This plant has an established root system and is ready for planting out

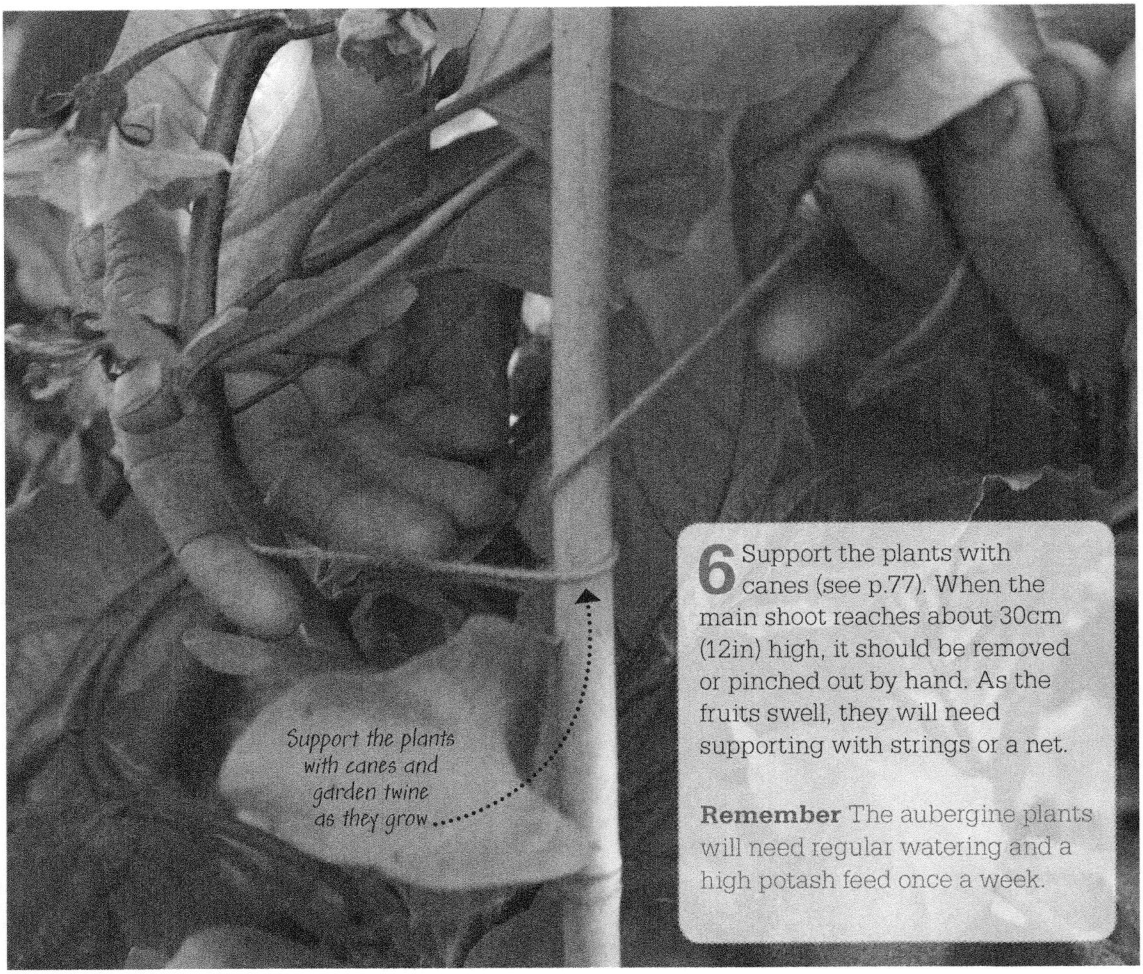

6 Support the plants with canes (see p.77). When the main shoot reaches about 30cm (12in) high, it should be removed or pinched out by hand. As the fruits swell, they will need supporting with strings or a net.

Remember The aubergine plants will need regular watering and a high potash feed once a week.

7 The stems can be tough and woody, so harvest the aubergines by cutting them from the plant with secateurs. Regular cutting will encourage further fruiting. Use aubergines quickly, as they don't keep well.

Careful! Don't leave the fruit on the plant for too long as the skin can turn dull and quickly overripen. Harvest when shiny.

Caring for your **Aubergines**

Aubergines are trickier to grow than many crops, but are well worth the effort – if you keep them healthy they can reward you with four to six fruits per plant.

When harvesting, leave part of the stem intact with the fruit.

Aubergines are heavy and need support to prevent damage to the plant

Harvesting the aubergines promptly allows the plant to concentrate its energy on those that are still growing

Things to watch out for...

Small fruits Regular watering will encourage the fruits to develop fully – it is important that plants receive a constant supply of water while the aubergines are swelling. Once the first flowers appear, start applying a high potash fertilizer rather than a general purpose feed, as this will encourage the fruits to form.

Sagging stems Aubergines are heavy fruits and so the plants will need regular staking and support with strings to ensure that the stems don't snap and cause damage to the crop.

Competing weeds Keep the area around the plant well weeded to prevent competition for water and nutrients. If you are growing the plants in the ground, hoe regularly around them.

Grow Asparagus

The young, tender spears of this delicious perennial plant are considered by many to be a gourmet treat. Patience is the key – the plant should not be harvested for at least three years, but the rewards will be worth the wait.

full sun | light soil

Equipment

- Asparagus crowns
- Well-rotted manure
- Spade
- Fork
- Rake
- Bamboo canes and string
- Scissors
- Watering can
- General-purpose liquid feed
- Asparagus knife

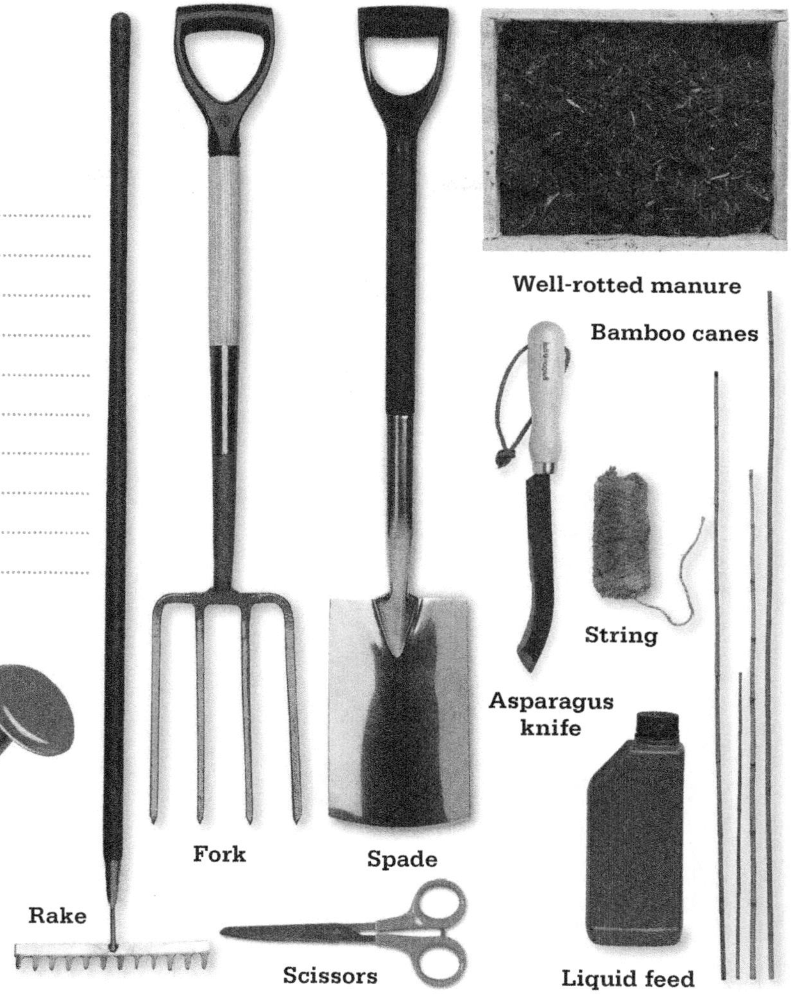

Asparagus *3 years until harvest*

Prepare *your site well before planting, in early spring*

Plant *the asparagus crowns into trenches in springtime*

After three years, *harvest for about 10 weeks in early spring*

1 It is very important to consider where you site your asparagus plants, as they can remain in the ground for up to 20 years. Dig in plenty of well-rotted manure or compost in the season before planting and make sure the ground is well prepared (see p.15).

Tip Asparagus plants can be grown from seed, but it is far easier to buy them as bare-root crowns in springtime.

Dig the ground over with a spade, ensuring that all perennial weeds are removed

Break up the soil well

2 Once your ground is thoroughly prepared, dig out a trench that is 30cm (12in) wide and 15cm (6in) deep. You can use a draw hoe or spade to do this.

Tip Sprinkle general-purpose compost into the bottom of the trench to give the plants a boost when they start to grow.

3 Create a mound on the floor of the trench. The peak of the ridge should be just below the level of the surrounding soil. Place the crowns on top of the ridge, 15cm (6in) apart, so that their tips are level with the soil's surface. Backfill the trench with soil.

Why? Growing the crowns on a mound helps drainage. If your soil is sandy then there is no need to plant in this way.

Spread the crowns on the mound, with the middle of the plant at the highest point

The crowns should fit comfortably within the width of the trench

Keep harvesting the spears for up to 10 weeks

Hold the spear carefully as you cut to prevent it snapping

4 Asparagus spears should only be harvested after they have been in the ground for more than three years. Any earlier, and the plants won't be able to establish roots and will die. Use an asparagus knife to cut the spears just below the level of the soil.

Tip Use secateurs if you don't have an asparagus knife.

Caring for your **Asparagus**

This luxury crop is easy to grow once established. If the ground is prepared thoroughly prior to planting, it should reward you with delicious spears for many years.

Things to watch out for...

Ferny foliage After 10 weeks of harvesting, stop to allow the plant's ferny foliage to develop. The foliage will turn yellow in autumn, at which point it should be cut down at ground level and added to the compost.

Asparagus beetle Keep an eye out for the bright-red asparagus beetle and remove by hand if you find it.

Sagging plants The tall foliage can be staked to prevent it flopping over other plants in the garden (see p.77).

Weeds Make sure you keep the asparagus beds weed free. They should also be mulched with organic matter each year in autumn to help retain moisture. Add a general-purpose fertilizer each spring.

Asparagus takes a few years to establish, but it's worth the wait

Grow Globe Artichokes

Globe artichokes are a delicious gourmet treat and their silvery, thistle-like plants will also make an attractive addition to the garden. Site them carefully, as these stately plants are a long term investment and should not be harvested until their second year.

full sun

moist soil

Equipment

- Globe artichoke seeds or offsets
- Seed trays
- General-purpose compost
- Propagator
- Plastic pots
- Watering can
- Fork
- Rake
- Well-rotted manure
- Secateurs

Watering can

Rake

Fork

Trowel

General-purpose compost

Propagator

Well-rotted manure

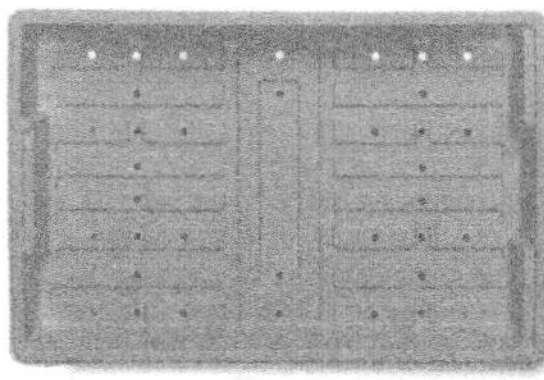
Seed trays

Secateurs

Plastic pots

Globe artichokes *1 year until harvest*

Sow *the seeds from late winter to spring and keep them warm*

Pot them on *in late spring after hardening off*

Harvest *the heads from late spring to early summer*

1 Sow the seeds 2cm (¾in) deep and the same distance apart. Water them in well, and keep warm. Once they have begun to develop they can be potted on.

Tip Although it is possible to raise globe artichokes from seed, or to buy them as cuttings from a mature plant, or "offsets", the simplest way to get started is to buy a young plant from a garden centre.

The seeds should be placed in a heated propagator to encourage germination

Place the plants outside during the day for 10 days to harden them off

2 The seedlings, whether you have bought them or grown them, will be ready to plant out in late spring. Harden them off (see p.74) and prepare the soil for them by removing all weeds and digging in plenty of well-rotted manure. Plant globe artichokes at a spacing of 1.5m (5ft). In the first few months, ensure that you keep the plants well watered to encourage them to establish strong roots.

3 The globe artichokes are ready to harvest once they reach about the size of an apple, but while the scales are still tight – over time these will begin to open to make way for the flowers. Cut the artichoke from the stem using a sharp knife or secateurs.

Tip The plant may produce buds on the sideshoots, and a second crop once you begin to harvest.

Take care when cutting as the stems are tough and woody

Use secateurs to make a clean cut through the thick stems

4 As globe artichokes are perennial plants and can last for several years it is important to take care of them over winter, as a strong frost can kill them. Cut the stems back to ground level and then cover the plant with a thick mulch of straw or bark chippings.

Tip In springtime, once the risk of frost has passed, simply move the mulch aside and dig it into the soil.

Caring for your **Globe artichokes**

This gourmet vegetable is well worth the effort, and once the plants are established they will provide you with delicious crops for several years.

Things to watch out for...

Blackfly This common pest can plague a globe artichoke plant, swarming the flower buds and stems, sucking the sap out and disfiguring new growth. Wash the pests from the plant if you can, and consider using an appropriate insecticide. Keep plants well fed and watered to help them recover. Generally globe artichokes are disease free.

Globe artichokes are stately plants and would make an attractive addition to a flowerbed

Create a Herb Parterre

A parterre is a formally designed herb, flower, or vegetable bed grown in a small space. Edged by evergreen hedges, they are typically grown using a palette of different shades of foliage and are an attractive and delicious addition to the garden. Choose your favourite herbs and create your own pattern.

full sun

light soil

Equipment

- Assorted herb plants, such as rosemary, lavender, thyme, and curry plant, a bay tree, and small box plants
- Horticultural grit
- Spade
- Rake
- Weed-suppressing membrane
- Gloves
- Measuring tape
- Chalk and short canes or pegs
- Stanley knife
- Trowel
- Slate chippings
- Watering can
- Secateurs

Gloves

Herb plants

Slate

Stanley knife

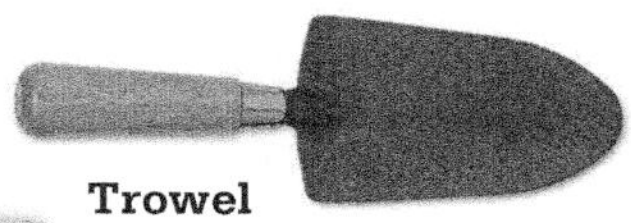

Trowel

Weed-suppressing membrane

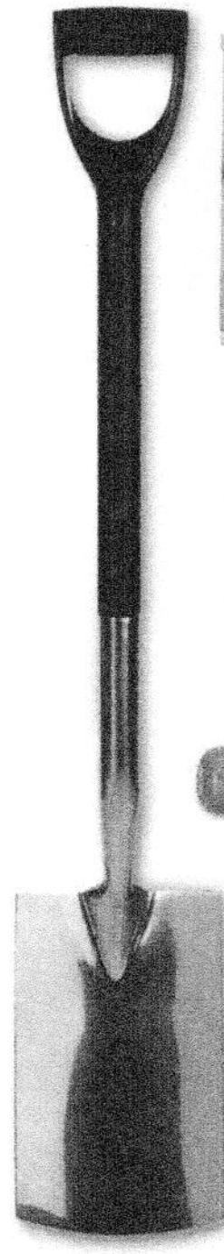

Spade

Rake

Secateurs

Horticultural grit

Herbs *4–16 weeks until harvest*

Prepare your soil *with grit in mid- to late spring*

Plant out *in late spring to early summer*

Pinch out *the growing box plants in midsummer*

Harvest *leaves as you need them throughout the year*

1 Herbs thrive in dry sites, which means that they need a free-draining soil. Dig over the soil and add about a bucket of grit per square metre (10sq ft) and dig it into the soil.

Remember Heavy clay soils will need extra attention and more grit, as water is very slow to drain through them (see pp.12–13).

2 After incorporating the grit, rake the soil level and remove any stones or weeds. The best tool for doing this job is a large-headed stainless steel landscape rake. Tread over the ground in both directions to remove any air pockets, and lightly rake again.

Careful! Remove any perennial weeds you come across, as any root pieces will quickly germinate.

3 Check that the area is now level – use a spirit level if you want to be exact – then lay a weed-suppressing membrane across the soil. This fabric should prevent weeds from germinating and preserve soil moisture, reducing your need to water.

Tip Use a spade to dig the edges of the fabric into the soil to hold it securely in place.

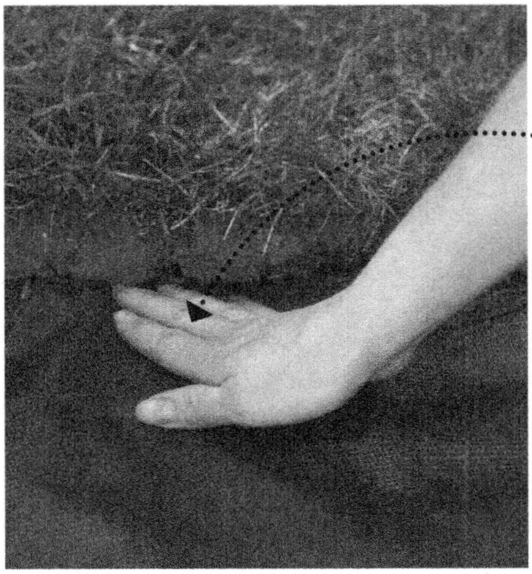

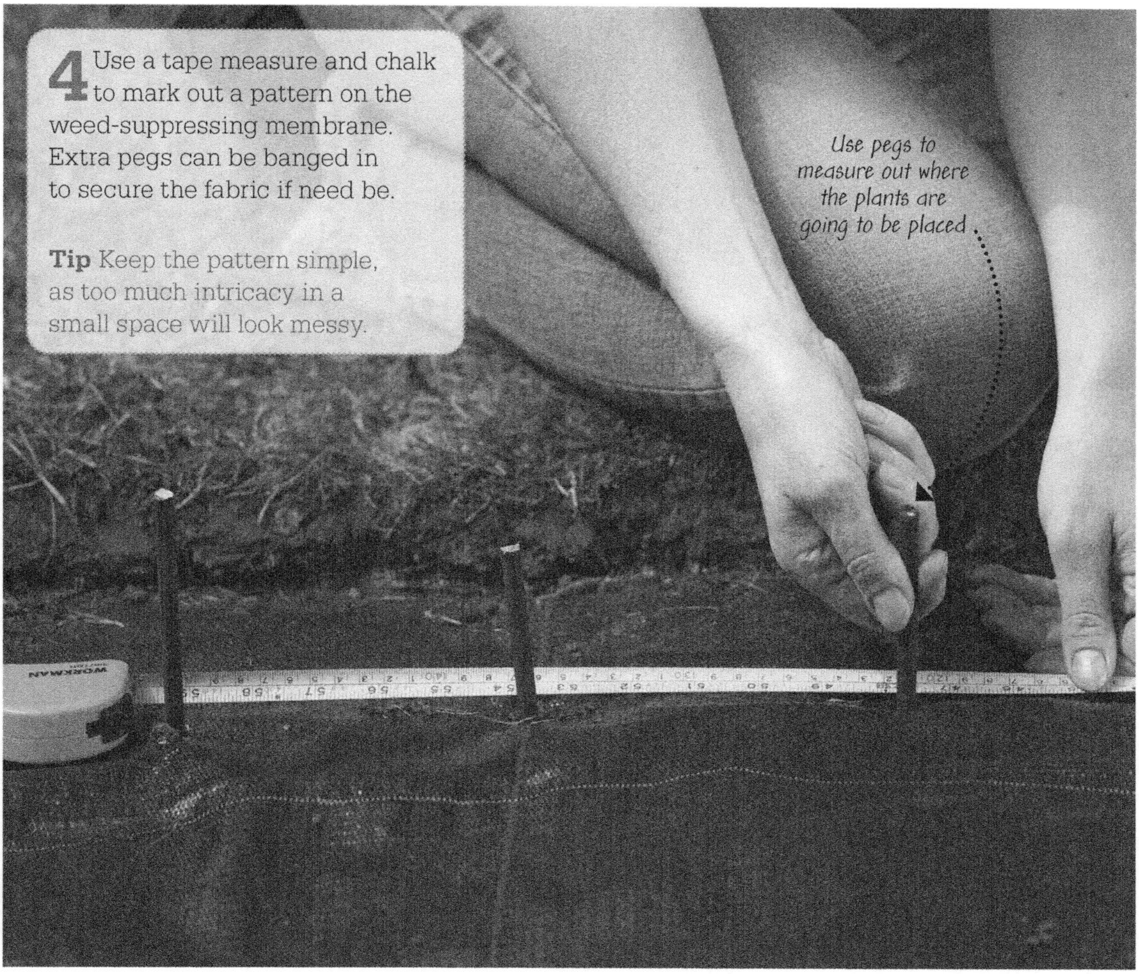

4 Use a tape measure and chalk to mark out a pattern on the weed-suppressing membrane. Extra pegs can be banged in to secure the fabric if need be.

Tip Keep the pattern simple, as too much intricacy in a small space will look messy.

5 Following your chalk pattern, use a sharp knife to create small planting holes in the fabric for the box edging plants – space them 20cm (8in) apart. Use a trowel to dig a hole in the soil underneath the membrane and plant them through it. Firm the plants in well with your fingers.

6 Continue to plant out the box hedging, following the pattern drawn on the fabric until all the plants are in the ground. Lay out the herb plants while they are in their pots. Play around with the positioning until you get an arrangement you are happy with.

Tip Use larger plants, such as the bay, in attractive terracotta pots to create a central focal point.

7 Once you are happy with the positioning of the herbs, plant them using the same technique given in step five. Use a brush to sweep the excess soil off the landscape fabric. Place slate chippings over the surface to hide the holes and create an attractive finish to the parterre.

Tip Trim back any leggy herbs by a third to encourage bushy growth.

Gravel or shingle can be used instead of slate

Caring for your **Herb Parterre**

The herb parterre is ideal outside a kitchen window. Once created, it should be easy to maintain and will provide a constant supply of herbs for the kitchen.

Lavender provides attractive flowers as well as aromatic foliage

Rosemary adds to the evergreen structure of the planting scheme

Box plants have been used to create this edging

Things to watch out for...

Weeds The landscape fabric laid over the planting beds should ensure that the parterre remains largely weed-free, but it will still need checking and weeding occasionally. Avoid using a hoe as this will rip the fabric.

Overwatering These herb plants come from the Mediterranean and will therefore require minimal watering once established. However, they will need watering for a few weeks after planting.

Missing mulch Look out for gaps in the slate mulch on the surface of the parterre; it will need topping up every couple of years.

Straggly plants Lavender and rosemary can be cut back lightly after flowering. Do not prune back into the older wood on lavender as it won't grow back. Box hedging should be clipped back neatly after the risk of frosts is over to keep these structural plants looking straight and formal.

Lawn edges If the parterre has been created in a lawn, the edges of the grass around the parterre will need regular cutting back to prevent it from encroaching on the plants.

Plant Blueberries in a Pot

Blueberries are ideal for containers – they need an acid soil and you can provide this far more easily if you grow them in a pot rather than in the open ground. Blueberries will produce an abundant crop of succulent, juicy berries and will also provide white spring flowers and a dazzling display of red and orange foliage in autumn.

full sun **light soil**

Equipment

- Blueberry plant
- Ericaceous compost
- Large container
- Crocks
- Watering can
  plants must be watered with rainwater to maintain the compost's acidity
- Sequestered iron feed

Ericaceous compost

Blueberry plant

Sequestered iron feed

Watering can

Crocks

Container

Blueberries *8–10 weeks until harvest*

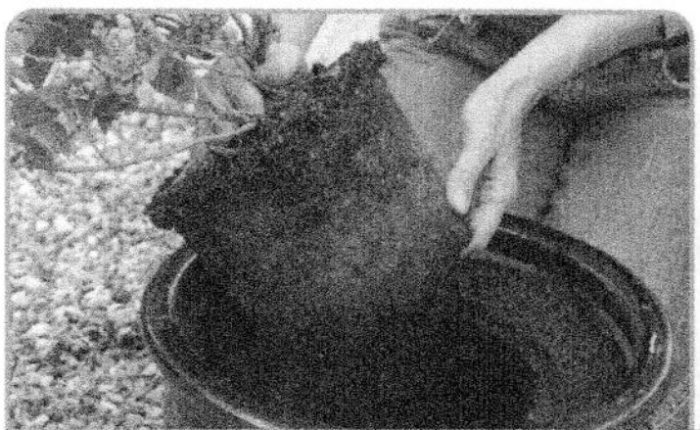

Pot up *your blueberry plants in either autumn or spring*

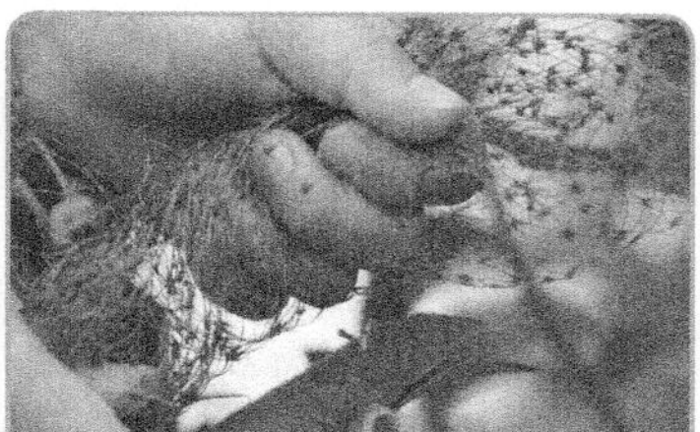

Protect *the fruit from birds, using netting as it ripens*

Harvest *the berries from late summer and into early autumn*

1 Remove the blueberry plant from its plastic pot and soak it in a bucket of rainwater for about 20 minutes prior to planting. Select an attractive-looking container about 38cm (15in) wide and cover the bottom with crocks for drainage. Put a layer of good-quality ericaceous compost in the bottom of the container and place the plastic pot on top of it. Fill around the pot with compost.

2 Push the compost around the pot and firm it down by hand. Make sure the compost is just below the rim of the container so that it will be level with the top of the blueberry's root ball.

Remember Before you plant the blueberry, move the pot to its final position in a sunny, sheltered spot. Once it is filled, it will be too heavy to move easily.

3 Remove the plastic pot from the container and place the plant in the hole created – the root ball will fit in perfectly. Ensure the top of the root ball sits level with the surface of the compost.

Careful! Do not mulch the top of the pot with manure as this can alter the acidity of the compost. Instead add a mulch of pebbles, gravel, slate, shells, or pea shingle.

4 Your plant will need netting in summer to prevent birds stealing the berries – construct a wigwam from attractive hazel or willow sticks (see pp.106–110) and hang the netting from this.

Careful! Plants need watering with rainwater as it is more acidic than tap water. To collect it, rig up a water butt to collect the runoff from a shed roof or house.

Ensure that the netting is secured at the bottom to keep out intruders

Caring for your **Blueberries**

Blueberries thrive in moist, acidic soil in full sun – ensure that you give them ericaceous compost and water them with rainwater to keep them happy and healthy.

Things to watch out for...

Garden thieves Birds can rapidly strip a plant of its berries and are the most likely threat to your crop, so make sure you rig up some netting to protect the plant when the fruit starts to ripen.

Spindly growth Lightly prune blueberry plants in early spring before they come into new growth. Remove some of the older wood at the base of the plant and cut back any dead or damaged growth (see pp.176–179 for further information).

Pick the berries when the fruit has turned blue

Also learn to grow ▶▶▶

How to grow **Strawberries in a Container**

full sun | **light soil**

Equipment

- 10 strawberry plants
- Terracotta strawberry planter
- General-purpose compost
- Crocks
- Slow-release compost
- Watering can

The trailing habit of strawberries makes them perfect for growing in planters. With good care, they should produce fruit for two or three years.

PLANTING

Buy strawberry plants in early spring. Place crocks over the drainage holes at the bottom of the planter and cover them up with a layer of compost that reaches just below the bottom level of planting holes. Place the strawberry plants through the planting holes so that their root balls sit inside the container. Once they are in position, add more compost until the second set of holes is reached and repeat the process. Finally, plant one or two strawberry plants in the top and firm in, ensuring that the compost level is just below the top of the container. Water in well. Be careful not to overfill the planter, as otherwise water will run straight off the surface when you water the plants.

LOCATION

Place the planter in a sheltered position on a patio in full sun. Stand the container on bricks, as this will help with drainage.

CARE

As soon as flowers start to appear on the plants they will need a weekly high-potash liquid feed, such as tomato fertilizer.

HARVESTING

The period of harvest depends on the type of strawberries. Summer-fruiting strawberries bear fruit from late spring to midsummer, depending on whether they are early, mid, or late varieties. Perpetual strawberries produce lighter crops but fruit throughout summer and into early autumn. Pick when the fruit turns red, retaining the stalk.

AFTER HARVESTING

Water the plants every day during summer. Ensure you give them a thorough soak, or the plants on the bottom level will remain dry. Old tatty foliage should be cut back with secateurs to expose the newer young foliage.

OVERWINTERING

Strawberries will benefit from being moved to a cool greenhouse during winter, or can grow on a porch or in a sheltered position. The plants should produce fruit for two or three more years, although yields will dwindle over time.

How to plant **a Pear Tree in a Pot**

full sun

light soil

Equipment

- A pear tree
- Large, deep container
- Soil-based compost
- Crocks
- Controlled-release fertilizer
- Secateurs

Pear trees are a beautiful addition to a garden, with their spring blossom and delicious, succulent fruit. Keeping the tree in a pot ensures that it stays small and compact, making picking the fruit easy.

PLANTING

Take the tree out of its pot and soak it in a bucket of water for an hour before planting. Add a layer of crocks to the bottom of the container and place a layer of compost on top. Tease out some of the roots before placing the tree in the container, ensuring that the top of the root ball sits about 5cm (2in) below the top of the pot.

Position the pear tree in the centre of the container and make sure it is upright and straight. Pack the compost around the root ball, making sure it comes up to the same level on the trunk as it did in the original pot. Water the tree in well.

CARE

Keep the tree well watered, especially during summer, when the pot will dry out quickly. Birds love to peck the ripening fruit, so cover the tree up with a net as the fruitlets start to develop. The tree should be re-potted into fresh compost every two or three years. Scrape at the root ball with a knife to stimulate new growth and add fresh fertilizer at the recommended rate. Mulch each year with manure.

HARVESTING

The tree should crop each summer. Be careful not to bruise the fruit when picking. Generally, pears are best picked when slightly underripe and allowed to ripen indoors, but check which variety you have to see whether fruit should be eaten immediately or is better stored for a few weeks.

PRUNING

Pear trees will benefit from a light prune each winter to encourage new growth. Remove crossing branches and anything that looks dead or diseased. Thin out the fruitlets in summer to encourage the tree to produce larger fruits.

Plant a Plum Tree

Delicious, juicy plums that can be eaten straight from the tree are a treat in summertime. Choose a self-fertile variety on a semi-dwarfing rootstock if you are short of space. You will need to protect your plum tree from frosts and prune it in spring or summer to keep it in shape.

full sun **moist soil**

Equipment

- Plum tree
- Fork
- Well-rotted manure
- Rake
- Tree stake and tree tie
- Watering can
- General-purpose liquid feed
- Secateurs

Well-rotted manure

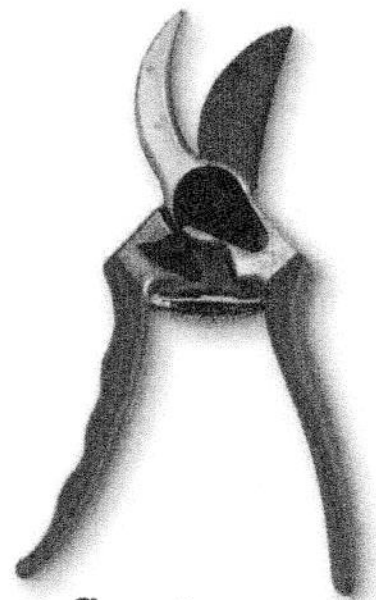

Secateurs

Watering can

Rake

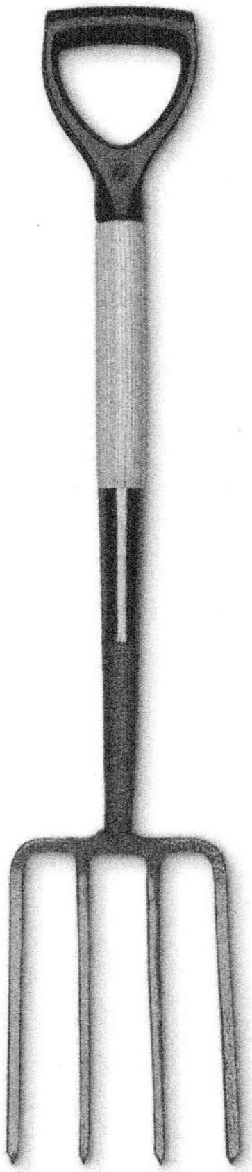

Fork

Tree stake

Tree tie

Liquid feed

Plums *14–16 weeks until harvest*

Plant *bare-root trees in autumn or spring; pot-grown all year*

Mulch *the tree with organic matter after planting in spring*

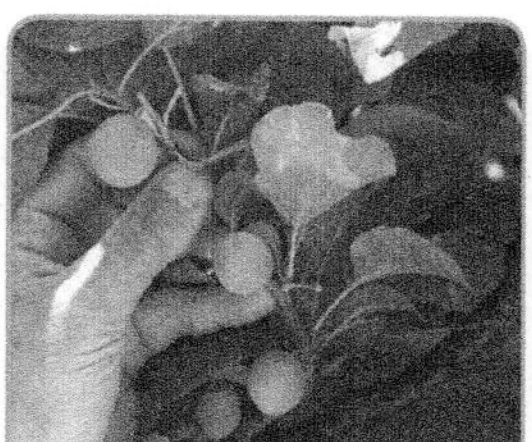

Thin out *the young fruitlets in early summer*

Harvest *the plump, ripe fruit in mid- to late summer*

1 Plum trees are best planted in autumn when the soil is still warm. This gives them a chance to settle before they start growing in spring. Dig a hole large enough to hold the root ball. Make sure the root ball is at the same level in the ground as it was in the pot. If it is planted too deeply, the trunk will rot; if too shallow, the root ball will dry out.

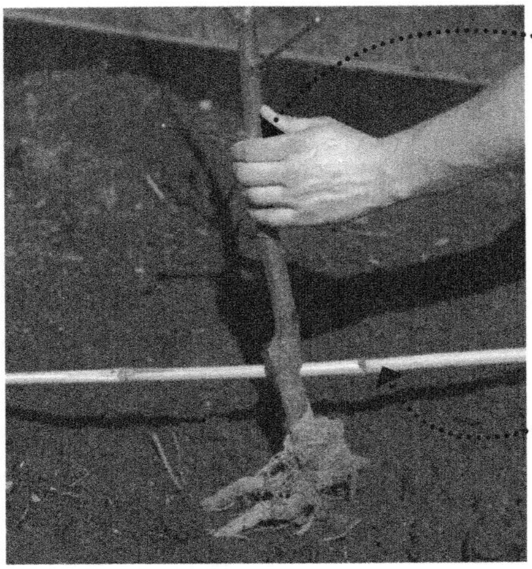

Make sure the tree is straight when planting it

Place a cane across the hole to get the top of the root ball level with the ground

2 Insert your tree stake before you plant your tree. Place the tree in the hole and fill around it using the soil you dug out – mix in some fertilizer as you do so, to ensure that the plant will be well-fed as it grows. Fix the tree firmly to the stake, using a tree tie.

Careful! It is vital to insert your stake in the ground before you plant your tree, otherwise you risk damaging the roots.

3 Once the tree is planted, add a layer of well-rotted manure or garden compost to the area above the root system. The layer should be about 5cm (2in) thick but should not be allowed to touch the trunk, as it may cause it to rot.

Why? This mulch will help retain moisture in the soil during the summer and suppress weeds.

Make sure the mulch is evenly scattered

Keep the mulch 5cm (2in) away from the trunk to prevent the tree rotting

4 New plum trees require regular watering until they are well rooted. Established trees are more drought-tolerant, but crop better if watered during dry spells. Mulch the tree again in spring with organic matter and apply a granular fertilizer.

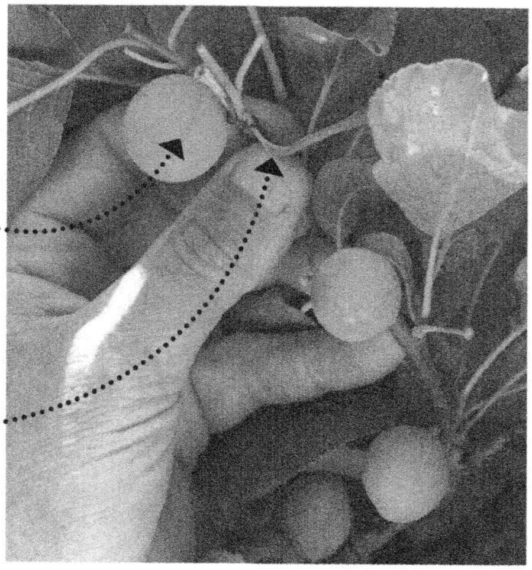

5 The plum tree should not be allowed to fruit for the first couple of years after planting, as you want it to first produce its roots and develop branches. This means that you will need to remove all the fruitlets when they appear.

Remember In subsequent years, fruit should be thinned in early summer – this will result in fewer but larger, better-quality fruits.

6 Fruit should be ready for picking between mid- to late summer, depending on the variety. Plums on the same tree may ripen at different times, so do a number of pickings on the same tree.

Careful! Never prune trees in wintertime. Wait for the buds to open before pruning in spring or late summer. Use secateurs to prune small branches and a pruning saw for the large ones.

Caring for your **Plum Tree**

Fresh plums are delicious in summer. With careful attention, a plum tree will make a beautiful and long-lasting addition to your garden.

Things to watch out for...

Dry soil Newly planted plums should be watered regularly during the summer. In subsequent years, they will only need watering during dry periods. Plum trees planted in the ground will benefit from a granular general-purpose feed spread around their root systems in spring, followed by an annual mulch of well-rotted manure around the base.

Frost The blossom can be damaged by frost as it starts to form in springtime. If possible, protect the tree by draping fleece over it at night.

Garden thieves The sweet ripening fruit is irresistible to birds, so throw a net over the tree in midsummer to prevent them from attacking the fruit. Wasps may also become a problem, so hang a jam jar filled with some jam and water nearby, to draw them away from your crop.

Crowded branches Plum trees should only be pruned when they are growing, in spring or summer. Never prune when the tree is dormant during winter, as the open wounds make it susceptible to disease. Remove any congested or damaged growth (see pp.176–179).

Also learn to grow ▸▸▸

How to plant a **Cherry Tree**

full sun **light soil**

Equipment

A cherry tree

Spade

Well-rotted manure

Tree stake and tie

Netting

General-purpose fertilizer

Secateurs

TREE SELECTION

If you are restricted for space, choose a self-fertile cherry tree such as 'Stella', as it will not need another tree for pollination; some varieties will not produce a crop without another tree nearby to fertilize them, so plan carefully. Make sure that the tree is on a dwarf rootstock such as colt or gisela 5 or 6. This will ensure it doesn't grow too big, which will make pruning and harvesting easier. Choose either a sweet cherry, as you can eat the fruit raw, or an acid cherry, whose fruit is good for cooking.

PLANTING

Select a sheltered, sunny spot. Dig out a hole double the width of the root ball and the same depth. Push in a vertical stake at the side of the hole. Place the tree in the hole and backfill with a mix of well-rotted manure and excavated soil; general-purpose fertilizer can also be mixed in. Mulch around the base of the tree and tie it to the stake using a tree tie. Water the tree well.

CARE

Don't allow the tree to fruit in the first two years – remove the young fruitlets by hand. This will give the tree time to develop a strong root system and branch structure. Harvest fruit in the third year. Use a net to protect the fruit from birds.

PRUNING

Sweet and acid cherries both need pruning in spring or summer, but have different pruning needs; it is important to know which type of tree you are dealing with or you may end up removing the fruit-bearing spurs by accident. Sweet cherries form fruit-bearing spurs on older wood, so leave some of this when pruning and cut back the newer growth by half to prevent congestion and a shady canopy. Acid cherries bear their fruit on wood produced the previous year. To prune an acid cherry, cut away some of the older wood and leave newer wood to produce fruit later that year.

Basic Pruning

Pruning should be carried out on woody plants such as trees and shrubs at least once a year, and sometimes two or three times, for a variety of reasons. It tidies up the plant, encourages fresh growth, relieves congestion, and allows sunlight to reach into the canopy. Most importantly, it allows you to remove dead, diseased, or dying branches.

Prune stone fruit trees such as plums, cherries, and peaches in summer

It is worth spending money on a good set of secateurs

Pruning wayward stems

Pruning to improve appearance

Pruning out crossing branches

Pruning congested plants

Fruit trees depend on sunlight to ripen their buds and produce a regular crop. Prune out crossing branches, as not only will they rub on each other, causing wounds and entry points for disease, but they also create too much shade. This will cause leggy growth at the expense of fruit. Ensuring that plants are not congested will also allow air to circulate around the canopy, which will help to prevent a build up of diseases such as mildew.

Split branches susceptible to disease

Using a pruning saw to remove diseased branches

Pruning diseased plants

Diseased branches may look corky, withered, pitted, or even have growths on them; foliage may be yellow, brown, mottled, or dead. If the affected branches are not removed promptly, they will pass on their infection to the rest of the plant and eventually kill it. Always make a clean pruning cut back to a healthy section of wood. When cutting away diseased material, make sure the saw or secateurs are sterilized afterwards to prevent the problem spreading.

Blueberries

Autumn-fruiting raspberries

Pruning for productivity

If left unpruned, plants may produce small, tasteless fruit and will eventually become a tangled mess of shoots and branches. It is important to keep fruit trees and bushes well-pruned so that sunlight can reach the fruiting buds – it promotes the formation and ripening of fruit. Careful pruning also encourages plants to produce a large crop, which will be easier to harvest from a well-tended plant. Different types of fruit require pruning in specific ways to maximize the amount of fruit they produce. For example, blueberries fruit on younger wood, so should be lightly pruned in winter or very early spring. You will need to remove some of the older branches and leave the majority of the younger wood on the plants. Alternatively, summer-fruiting raspberries should have their old canes removed at ground level after fruiting, leaving just the new canes in place, while autumn-fruiting raspberries should have all their stems cut to ground level in early spring. In spring, new shoots will emerge. Always check your plant's needs before you prune.

The weaker fruit fall during the "June drop", allowing the tree to concentrate on growing the strongest fruit

Fallen fruit should be removed immediately before it attracts wasps and harbours diseases

The "June drop"

In midsummer, trees naturally shed some of their fruit. This ensures they don't overcrop and exhaust themselves. It also prevents their branches from becoming overladen with heavy fruit and snapping. Once the drop is finished, fruit can be thinned again, if necessary.

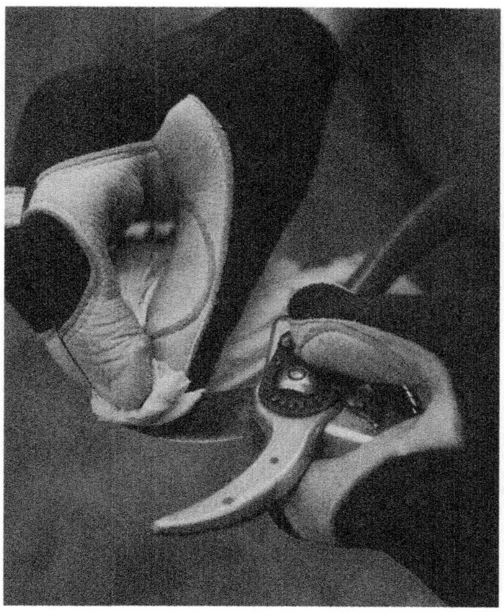

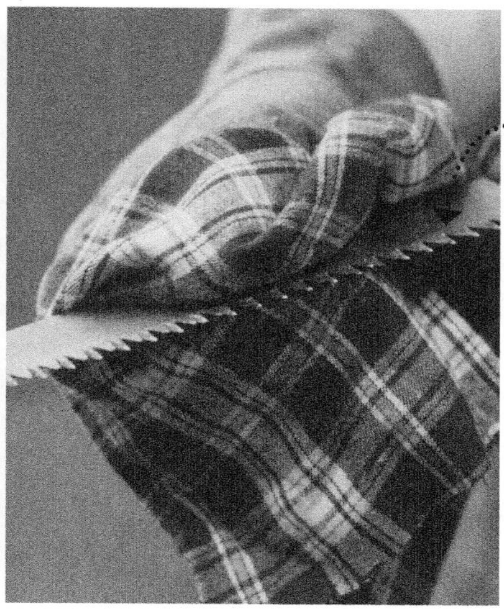

After pruning, use an oily rag to remove the sap and sawdust from the teeth of the blade

Caring for your tools

Clean your tools with household disinfectant before and after each use to avoid spreading diseases from one plant to the other. Wipe saws with an oily rag and sharpen secateurs by rubbing a sharpening stone across the blade, to ensure a clean cut when pruning.

Pruning Forms

If you fancy becoming a first-class gardener, why not train your fruit trees into different shapes? A trained tree takes up less space and can bear more fruit than a free-standing type. All you need are the right timings and techniques. Here are some of the more commonly seen styles.

Tip Cordons that are tilted at 45 degrees are called oblique cordons, and produce an equal amount of fruit along the trunk. The advantage of cordons is that you can grow lots of different varieties in a small space.

Cordons

These grow on a single stem with short, stubby fruiting spurs along their length. Cordons should be pruned in late summer. Prune back the new growth to one or two buds but allow the leading shoot to grow until it has reached the desired height. This technique means that varieties that bear fruit on the tips would lose their fruit for the next year, so select tree varieties that produce fruit on spurs and not on the tips of new growth.

These branches need supporting with a system of wires

Prune the new growth back to two buds in late summer

Espaliers

An espalier has a central trunk with a series of parallel horizontal tiers growing out from it. It adds a wonderful ornamental value to the garden. You can create as many tiers as you like, if the vigour of the tree is capable, although most commonly there are four or five. Prune in late summer, cutting back the new growth to two buds from the branches.

Unlike cordons and espaliers, standard apple trees should be pruned in winter

Choose a dwarfing rootstock to keep the tree small and compact

Half standards

This is the most commonly seen tree shape. Half standards have a small branch-free leg about 50cm (20in) high. Above this, the canopy branches out into the shape of an open-centred goblet. Prune when the tree is dormant, in winter. To keep the open shape, remove any crossing stems in the centre of the tree to allow sunlight into the canopy.

Store Carrots in Soil

Carrots are easy to grow, but keeping them crunchy and fresh over winter can be a little trickier – once they have been dug up, it is important to store them as quickly as possible as the air can cause them to go soft.

1 If stored correctly, carrots can be kept in a cardboard box for a few months. All you will need is a sturdy cardboard box, some old newspaper, and some soil-based compost. Remove all the green leaves and foliage on the carrots, as these will draw moisture away from the root. Place a layer of newspaper and a 2.5-cm (1-in) thick layer of compost into the box.

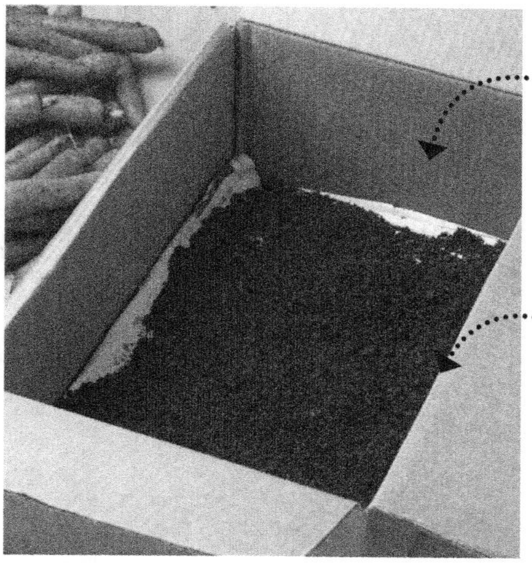

Place newspaper or kitchen paper in the bottom of the box first

Avoid using soil from your garden that could have pests and slugs in it

Space carrots out evenly in the box ensuring they don't touch each other

2 Doublecheck the carrots for any defects or diseased parts. One bad carrot can quickly rot and contaminate the rest of the crop. Lay the carrots on the soil, spacing them out so that they are not in contact with each other.

3 Cover the first layer of carrots with another layer of compost, also 2.5cm (1in) thick. Place another layer of carrots on top and repeat this process until the box is full.

Careful! The cardboard box should be stored in a cool, well-ventilated, rodent-free place such as a shed or garage.

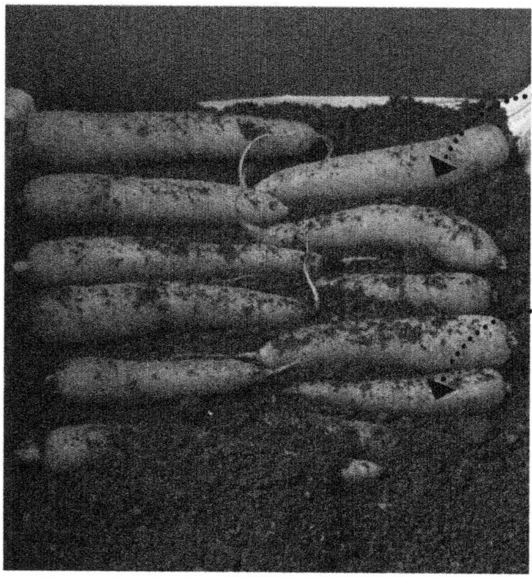

Keep creating layers of carrots until you reach the top of the box

Once placed in storage it should be checked regularly for rotting crops

How to **Store Crops**

WRAPPING IN PAPER

Apples will keep for a few months if wrapped in paper and kept in a cool, dark place. Some varieties of apples store better than others, so check before you harvest. Use tissue paper to prevent the fruit becoming damaged in storage – any cuts or bruises will quickly cause the fruit to rot. Alternatively, lay the apples out on trays so that their skins aren't touching. Check the fruit regularly to ensure that it hasn't started to rot.

Storing apples in paper

DRYING

You can dry fruit and vegetables in different ways: a variety of crops such as apples, plums, parsnips, and tomatoes can be dried in the oven on a very low heat, while crops such as beans, chillies, and herbs can be air-dried.

To oven-dry apples, wash, core, and slice them into rings and rinse them in 600ml (1 pint) water with 2 tbsp lemon juice mixed in. Dry the rings off on a tea towel and then arrange them on wire cooling racks placed on baking trays. Place them in the oven for between 8–24 hours on the lowest heat, turning them occasionally. Once you are happy with the texture, remove them from the oven, leave them to stand for a few hours, and then seal them in an airtight container.

To air-dry chillies, harvest the peppers with a small amount of stem attached. Knot them onto a string and hang them up in a warm, dry place for a few weeks, until they are shrivelled.

Drying apples

MAKING JAMS AND PRESERVES

Cooking and bottling your excess crops is another excellent way of storing them, especially if you have a glut of crops that you don't want to waste. Almost any fruit or vegetable can be converted into a delicious jam or chutney, so find a recipe that takes your fancy, and get cooking!

STORING IN SACKS

Root crops such as potatoes will store well if they are dried, placed in double layered paper sacks, and kept in a cool, frost-free place. Make sure that the tubers are completely dry before you store them, to prevent them from rotting. Ensure that light is not allowed to reach them.

Alternatively, root crops such as swedes can be stored in a homemade "clamp". In a sheltered corner of your garden, lay a thick layer of straw on the ground and pile your crops on top of it to create a pyramid. Cover this over with straw and then pack soil on top of it to keep the roots warm. Check the crops every now and then for signs of damage.

Storing potatoes in a sack

FREEZING

Some fruits and vegetables can be frozen if you have a glut and enough room in your freezer to keep them. Some fruit can be frozen whole, such as raspberries, blackcurrants, redcurrants, and blueberries. Strawberries will only be usable for purées, jams, or sauces after freezing. Fruit such as apples and pears need to be made into a purée before you freeze them.

To freeze blueberries, wash the fruit thoroughly and remove any that looks diseased. Spread the fruit out on a baking tray, so that none of the berries are touching, and place it in the freezer. Once the fruit has frozen solid, transfer it into clean containers such as plastic boxes or polythene bags and store it in these. Freezing the fruit this way means that the berries will not freeze into a solid lump, and can be used individually once defrosted – you may feel this is unnecessary if you only intend to use the fruit for cooking.

Vegetables such as beans and broccoli will need to be blanched quickly before freezing. Boil them in water for a few minutes until soft and then immerse them in ice water to cool them quickly. Dry them off and then place in the freezer.

Freezing blueberries

Index

About the Author

Simon Akeroyd is the Garden and Countryside Manager at Polesden Lacey, Surrey and was previously a Garden Manager for the Royal Horticultural Society. He has worked as a BBC horticultural researcher and journalist. He is the author of *Simple Steps Lawns and Ground Cover, Simple Steps Shrubs and Small Trees*, and the co-author of *The Allotment Handbook* and *Grow Your Own Fruit*.

Acknowledgements

Photographic Credits

Dorling Kindersley would like to thank **Peter Anderson** for new photography.

pp.18 (left); **105**; **128** (top); **129** (centre): **Alan Buckingham** © Dorling Kindersley.

All other images © Dorling Kindersley.

For further information see www.dkimages.com

Publisher's Acknowledgements

Special thanks are due to **Squires Garden Centres** who kindly lent gardening tools for the photoshoots.

Dorling Kindersley would also like to thank:

2013 edition credits
In UK

Written by Simon Akeroyd

Project Editor Becky Shackleton
Project Art Editor Gemma Fletcher
Design assistance Jessica Bentall, Alison Gardner, Elaine Hewson, Vicky Read
Senior Editor Alastair Laing
Indexer Chris Bernstein
Managing Editor Penny Warren
Managing Art Editor Alison Donovan
Art Directors Peter Luff, Jane Bull
Publisher Mary Ling

DK Images Claire Bowers, Freddie Marriage, Emma Shepherd, Romaine Werblow

Loan of gardening tools Squires Garden Centres

At Tall Tree Ltd
Editor Rob Colson
Designer Malcolm Parchment

In India
Design assistance Ranjita Bhattacharji, Devan Das, Tanya Mehrotra, Ankita Mukherjee
Senior Art Editor Ivy Roy
Art Editors Prashant Kumar, Karan Chaudhary
Editors Suefa Lee, Vibha Malhotra
Editorial assistance Swati Mittal
Senior Editor Garima Sharma
Managing Editor Alka Thakur Hazarika
Deputy Managing Art Editor Priyabrata Roy Chowdhury
DTP Designers Rajesh Singh Adhikari, Sourabh Chhallaria, Arjinder Singh
CTS/DTP Manager Sunil Sharma

Printed in Great Britain
by Amazon

37701355R00113